Pape.

Paper Pilgrimage

Keeping a Personal
and Spiritual Journal

LAWRENCE OSBORN

Foreword by Joyce Huggett

daybreak
London

First published in 1990 by
Daybreak
Darton, Longman and Todd Ltd
89 Lillie Road, London SW6 1UD

British Library Cataloguing in Publication Data

Osborn, Lawrence
    Paper pilgrimage.
    1. Christian life. Role of diaries
    I. Title   II. Series
    248.4

ISBN 0–232–51855–6

Phototypeset by Input Typesetting Ltd,
London SW19 8DR
Printed and bound in Great Britain by
Courier International Ltd, Tiptree, Essex

Contents

Foreword

This is quite the most helpful, imaginative and practical book on keeping a spiritual journal that I have yet come across and although I claimed to be a dedicated journal keeper before reading *Paper Pilgrimage*, I felt full of fresh enthusiasm and inspiration by the time I had finished reading Lawrence Osborn's manuscript.

Many others, I believe, will thank God for this timely book: those who have often longed to begin a prayer journal but haven't known quite how to start; those who have had stabs at keeping a journal but, in the absence of the kind of creative help contained here, have given up; and those who want to learn how to trace some of the ways God has been at work in their lives without falling into the trap of becoming unduly introspective. But the book will not only appeal to individuals concerned to deepen their prayer life, prayer groups will benefit from working through some of the exercises together. Retreat givers and spiritual directors, too, will find here a wealth of ingenious exercises, which, given to the right retreatant at the right time, could produce prolific growth.

I shall certainly be drawing on the insights gleaned from this book both for myself and with the groups and individuals who give me the privilege of journeying alongside them on the path of prayer.

Joyce Huggett

Preface

Many people already keep some form of journal. Many more have tried and failed, or are vaguely aware that other Christians seem to derive great benefit from the practice. I have written this book for all who want to do more with their journal, or who would like to try again, or who would like to keep a journal but don't really know where to begin.

The following chapters are primarily a collection of hints and further resources for the would-be journal keeper. They are not a theoretical analysis or critique of the practice of keeping a journal. Nor do I presume to offer a set of rules for 'successful' journal keeping. All the exercises have been used successfully either in my own journal or in spiritual journal workshops. However, you will almost certainly find some parts of the book more helpful than others. By all means use the parts you enjoy or feel you can benefit from and disregard the rest.

1

The Many Faces of the Journal

'I have often felt a motion of love to leave some hints in writing of my experience of the goodness of God, and now, in the thirty-sixth year of my age, I begin this work.'

Thus John Woolman began his journal. Many people begin journal keeping because of a conscious decision of this sort. Maybe they feel it is important to keep a record of their lives or perhaps they turn to the journal as a means of recollection and self-discipline. For others, journal keeping may flow naturally out of a life-long tendency to write everything down.

I fall into the second type. The prehistory of my journal dates back to my seventh birthday. I was given a five-year diary bound in red imitation leather, with a brass lock, and an inch of space for each entry. I began my journal with enthusiasm, faithfully recording as much of my life as I could squeeze into the space available. But I felt obliged to write in it every day and I felt guilty when I forgot. I began inventing entries to fill the gaps and even resorted to filling them in with comments about the weather. Gradually my journal keeping lapsed and in later years I used the diary to keep lists of books that I wanted to read (I didn't realise that such lists were also journal entries).

In spite of that false start, the desire to keep a

journal remained with me. As a teenager, I graduated to large hardback business diaries acquired from my father. However, I found that as I progressed through school and university any personal reflections I might commit to the pages of those diaries were swamped by elaborate programmes of work and revision.

My conversion to Christianity stimulated my return to the idea of a personal journal as opposed to a work log. I began reading missionary biographies and realised that many of the people about whom I was reading must have kept diaries. They found it beneficial, why shouldn't I?

I was surprised to find that the idea had little support amongst Christian friends. Someone I respected told me, 'I used to keep a diary as a teenager. Of course, I don't do that now.' I got the impression that keeping a personal journal was a sign of spiritual immaturity, that it was symptomatic of an unhealthy interest in oneself or an inflated idea of one's own importance. The true disciple puts aside such delusions of grandeur. In spite of that climate I persevered for a while until, in a mood of over-zealous humility, I burned all my old journals!

Some years later, I came across a book entitled *Keeping Your Personal Journal* (written by a Roman Catholic priest, George Simons). That book galvanised me into beginning again. It taught me that writing can be a valuable spiritual discipline. Since then I have kept a journal more or less continuously and have become convinced of its value in my life. It is a way of putting my experiences in perspective, of affirming and expressing myself creatively, and, above all, of encountering God.

But what precisely is a journal? This question is more difficult to answer than one might imagine. In later chapters I shall try to answer it in a practical way. For now, let me outline for you something of the diversity of published journals.

'THIS IS NOT A BOOK'!

Paul Gauguin began his journal with these words, and repeated them whenever he felt he was in danger of forgetting the purpose of his writing. A personal diary or journal is not a book. It is not a piece of literature or a work of art. The normal rules and conventions of writing do not apply to the journal.

The most basic difference is that a journal, unlike a book, is incomplete. It is incomplete because it reflects the incompleteness of my life. Newman once remarked that the only evidence of life is growth. My biological growth may be over but, hopefully, my personal and spiritual growth will never cease. The personal journal is a reflection of that endless process.

Since the journal reflects the process that is me, it has often been described as a mirror. In its pages we may find a moving image which represents who I have been, who I now am, and who I am becoming.

Keeping a journal has also been likened to embarking on a voyage of self-discovery. In its pages we may record the landmarks of our inner landscape. It helps us to recollect where we have been in the journey of our soul. It puts the present in context and may be used to give direction to where we go next. Commenting in his diary, Henri Nouwen says, 'I have little to say about events, good or bad, creative or destructive, but much about the way I

3

remember them – that is, the way I start giving them form in the story of my life.'[1]

Thus the journal is my own personal guide-book to where I have been both in everyday life and in the inner life of my soul and spirit. Seen in these terms it is a tool to be used rather than a work of literature to be read.

The personal journal may also be likened to a butterfly net. My journal is a trap in which I can catch and hold on to otherwise fleeting thoughts, feelings, insights, experiences, dreams and fantasies. Many of them have no meaning for anyone except myself. However, others have had very practical implications. It has been an invaluable aid in my research and my writing. Indeed the book you are now reading has its ultimate origin in observations in my journal.

Throughout this book I shall talk about journals rather than diaries. At one level the words are interchangeable: my dictionary defines them both as a 'daily record of events'. However, 'diary' suggests to me a pre-printed book with a fixed amount of space for each day and, perhaps, for appointments every half-hour. On the other hand, 'journal' suggests something more personal and flexible than a diary. It reminds me, of the word 'journey': the record of my journey through life. Bishop John Robinson felt the same way. He described his journal as 'something very different from a diary, which has always oppressed me. There you feel you have got to record something every day, whether there is something worth saying or not . . .'[2]

1. Henri Nouwen, *The Genesee Diary: Report from a Trappist Monastery*, p. 160.
2. Quoted in Eric James, *A Life of Bishop John A. T. Robinson: Scholar, Pastor, Prophet*, Collins, p. 285.

The shelves of any public library or bookshop bear witness to the fact that journal keeping has been deeply attractive to many people in recent centuries. We have access to the personal journals of an incredible variety of famous and infamous men and women. As a result, virtually the entire range of human endeavour is available to us in this form.

The chronicle

Most people on hearing the word 'journal' tend to think of a chronological account of those events (both public and private) which the writer considers worthy of recollection. Along with memoirs and biographical works, such chronicles were the mainstay of historical writing before the appearance of professional historians.

We generally think of them as the works of individuals, such as Samuel Pepys, but this need not be the case. Originally chronicles traced significant events in the life of a nation or other group of people from a particular perspective. The Anglo-Saxon Chronicle was the official history of England before the Norman Conquest. Its authors were expected to justify the actions of the community and generally enhance the group's sense of a common identity.

Other public chronicles were written from a particular religious perspective. Thus the Old Testament Books of Samuel and Kings were written in order to illustrate that the well-being of Israel was intimately bound up with the faithfulness of its people and particularly its leaders to Yahweh. Similarly one of the functions of the Acts of the Apostles was to illustrate the role of the Holy Spirit in the development of the early church.

The idea of a community chronicle need not be limited to a nation or a religion. Journals have been kept on behalf of smaller groups such as individual villages, religious communities and churches. It is also possible to maintain a family journal; Dietrich Bonhoeffer's father kept such a journal for many years. Such a journal could be the exclusive task of one member of the family, community or congregation (Edith Schaeffer speaks of being the curator of the family's memories) or it could be a large scrapbook to which everyone contributes.

The commonplace book

Quite different from the chronicle but, nevertheless, closely associated with the journal is the commonplace book. This is a storehouse or junkroom filled with favourite quotations, maxims, jokes, anecdotes, and proverbs to live by. It is a basket of (literary) fragments united by the interest they have aroused in their collector. The fragments may be the work of the collector or they may come entirely from things he or she has read or heard. Entries may be undated and may also neglect to mention the source from which they were gleaned.

Such collections have many uses. Dag Hammarskjöld's *Markings* appears to have been a summary of his personal philosophy. I know of an evangelist who uses such a book as a treasure trove of anecdotes, stories and quotations to illustrate speeches and sermons. Many professional writers rely on such 'idea books' for ideas, characters, descriptions, portraits, the raw material for poems, etc.

Travel journals

Journal keeping has also been pressed into the service of a wide variety of more specialised purposes. The commonest of these is probably the travel or holiday journal. At one time every young man or woman who went on holiday felt obliged to keep such a record. In spite of the general availability of cheap and easy to use cameras many people still like to keep a written record of their holidays. An interesting contemporary example of what can be done with a holiday journal is Marion Milner's *Eternity's Sunrise*.

Of course this is easier to do when you have time to relax. The average package tour or activity holiday simply doesn't provide me with sufficient space for journal keeping. On the other hand, an entire volume of my journal is devoted to three relatively unprogrammed months I once spent in Israel.

The travel journal has its professional counterpart in the logbooks of navigators and explorers. While some of these make dry and academic reading others succeed in bringing the experiences of the explorer to life. The journals of Captain Scott (published as *Scott's Last Expedition*) are a particularly moving example of this type of journal.

The nature journal

Like the travel journal this focusses mainly on the author's amateur or professional observations of the world. A nature journal is simply a chronological record of some aspect of the living world (hence the term natural *history*). Well-known examples include Gilbert White's *Natural History of Selborne* and Charles Darwin's *The Voyage of the 'Beagle'* (which demonstrates the close connection between travel and nature journals by combining the two in one).

The inward-looking journal

Other journal keepers focus on their own inner world rather than on the details or events of the world about them.

Journal keeping has often been used as a way of coping with traumatic experiences. Many people find that the discipline of writing helps them come to terms with such experiences. Thus many well-known journals owe their inspiration to some sort of life crisis.

For some people the stimulus is provided by chronic or terminal illness. Alice James, the invalid sister of Henry and William James, kept such a journal. It became a place where she could express her creativity and face the inevitability of premature death.

Keeping a journal is also a common response to bereavement. This was what motivated C. S. Lewis's *A Grief Observed*. He set out to make a map of his sorrow at the death of his wife. Through the process of keeping this journal he not only came to terms with his grief but achieved fresh insights into his own personality.

Another stimulus to journal keeping has been the experience of oppression. Sadly this century has produced a rich crop of such journals. Perhaps the best known are personal records of suffering under the Nazis such as that of Etty Hillesum.

In this century the use of the journal as a tool for the conscious exploration of one's beliefs and psyche has received fresh impetus from the development of psychoanalysis. Carl Jung's encounter with his own unconscious (and the system of psychoanalysis which developed as a result) was aided by keeping a journal of his dreams and fantasies. This practice has been taken up and formalised by the American analyst, Ira Progoff, who is perhaps the best known advocate of journal keeping as a tool for self-realisation. A less formal approach, but one also influenced by Jung, is that of the English psychoanalyst Marion Milner.

An alternative approach (which places more emphasis on the journal as an aid to personal creativity) has been inspired by the work of Otto Rank. Its clearest literary expression is the diary of Anaïs Nin. An account of this approach can be found in *The New Diary* by Nin's disciple and colleague Tristine Rainer.

As a result of this fresh interest the journal has been rediscovered as an important tool in the search for selfhood in our increasingly fragmented society: a search which for the post-war generation was symbolised by the diary of Anne Frank and which, more recently, has been satirised by Sue Townsend in *The Secret Diary of Adrian Mole*.

Alternatives

Not everyone keeps a journal but many people engage in alternative activities which offer similar benefits. The most obvious alternative is letter writing. A lengthy correspondence with someone you trust is similar in many ways to a personal journal. Indeed the similarities are even closer when you recall that many journals are couched in the form of unsent letters. Some journal keepers endow their journals with a personality, e.g., Anne Frank addressed her journal entries to Kitty. Other journal keepers address their journals to some person: a parent, a close friend, their future self.

Another activity which has parallels with journal keeping is autobiography. Like the journal, the autobiography is a voyage of self-discovery. Unlike the journal, it has a definite destination. If the journal is a moving image of one's life, the autobiography may be likened to a portrait painted from some particular perspective in time. Autobiography is often approached as a work of literature rather than a tool for personal growth. Thus it tends to be written with its potential readership in mind.

Nevertheless there is considerable overlap between the two. A journal may provide most of the raw material for an autobiography. Conversely, short autobiographies may appear as major entries in a journal: the introductory chapter of John Woolman's journal is a summary of his life prior to beginning the journal. Indeed it is quite conceivable for a personal journal to consist exclusively of short autobiographies written at different times.

Yet another alternative to the journal is the photograph album. Many people keep photographs which aid their recollection of the significant people, places and events in their lives. Used systematically this could become a visual journal to complement the more traditional form of journal. An extension of this to include other memorabilia leads us to the scrapbook. This is often dismissed as an exercise in nostalgia. However, for some personality types the scrapbook or photograph album may offer a more satisfying means of self-discovery than the traditional journal.

Given the many uses to which journals have been put, it is not surprising to find that they have also been used to record or evoke religious experiences and spiritual growth. Of course, the keeping of spiritual journals is by no means restricted to Christians. A similar practice thrived in Japan before the arrival of the first Christian missionaries, while in western Europe some of the earliest journal keepers were not Christians but witches.

There are forms of religious experience, such as possession (whether by subconscious or external psychic forces), which are not compatible with faith in the God and Father of our Lord Jesus Christ. Journal exercises designed to evoke such experiences have no place in a Christian spiritual journal.

The spiritual journal is a technique which many Christians have found helpful in the course of their journeys with God. However, like every other technique in this sphere it is no guarantee of spiritual growth. There is nothing automatic about it that could somehow absolve us of our personal responsibility or of the need for complete reliance on the grace of God.

Criticisms

The practice of keeping a spiritual journal is not without its critics. A few very conservative Christians are inclined to condemn any religious practice that is not explicitly advocated in the pages of the New Testament. They seem to believe that whatever is not commanded must be forbidden. Quite apart from the questionability of this stance, the objection that journal keeping is unbiblical is simply anachronistic. Since it did not exist in biblical times, lack of biblical references to journal keeping is not sufficient reason for condemning the practice.

A more serious objection is that the spiritual journal's emphasis on your own religious experience is incorrigibly self-centred. Many Christians regard focussing upon the self as central to human sinfulness. While there is some truth in this, it does not follow that the spiritual journal necessarily encourages an inordinate attention to one's own spiritual state. In my journal, I often address letters to God. If these are genuine attempts to communicate my thoughts, feelings and experiences, I find that the discipline of writing such letters redirects my attention away from myself to God.

Another serious criticism is that of the veteran exponent of journal keeping, Ira Progoff. He warns that the use of a journal to achieve a closer relationship with God actually places restrictions on the personal processes that can be encouraged by journal keeping. In other words, it limits the possibilities of personal growth that may result from the journal. My response to this is that if a God-centred journal restricts personal growth it is not because it is God-centred but because it is centred on the wrong God. The God of Christianity is not one who restricts our growth. That was a lie put about by nineteenth-century humanist critiques of religion (e.g., the writings of Feuerbach, Marx, and Freud). On the contrary, the God revealed by Jesus is the one who gives sight to the blind and sets the captives free. Keeping a journal as a Christian discipline ought to be a radically liberating process; one that brings new freedom both in the spiritual and the personal spheres.

On a more positive note, I believe that the Bible provides us with certain precedents for the keeping of spiritual journals. While it is true that the biblical authors never envisaged individual spiritual journals, they clearly advocate the recollection of what God has done for you. The mighty acts of God were recited in the hearing of the Israelites (e.g., Neh. 8:1–3); the kings of Israel were expected to make their own copy of the Books of Moses on ascension to the throne (Deut. 17:18); and God's dealings with humankind both individually and corporately were central to the praise and worship of Old and New Testament believers.

Insofar as it is a powerful aid to such recollection, journal keeping is a legitimate response to these exhortations. St Paul also exhorts us to meditate on whatever is true, honourable, just, pure, lovely, and gracious (Phil. 4:8): a journal can be an invaluable aid to such meditation.

Another precedent for journal keeping as a Christian discipline is set by the Christian traditions of spiritual biography and autobiography. Beginning with Augustine and perpetuated by many of the great saints of the Christian Church this practice has provided us with written records of the many and various ways in which God has encountered his people over the centuries. Nor has the practice died out in the twentieth century. To this day Christians find that the need to tell others about what God has done for them leads them to set their story down in writing. If others can benefit from our experiences can we not do so ourselves? The spiritual journal offers us a continuing record of the ways in which God has been working in our lives. As such, it is a sourcebook for praising God and to testifying of his grace.

Many of the founding fathers of evangelicalism found it helpful to keep such journals. John Wesley's journal is probably the best known but many of his contemporaries and co-workers also kept spiritual journals. The practice continued to flourish amongst evangelicals in the nineteenth century. The great evangelical leader Charles Simeon kept a journal as did many of those he influenced, including the pioneer missionary, Henry Martyn. Journal keeping was also popular amongst Christians of other traditions: John Newman kept a journal, and from the continent come such classics as the *Journals* of Kierkegaard.

In our own century the practice of keeping a spiritual journal has become less widespread (as, indeed, has secular journal keeping). However, some Christian leaders maintain the tradition. Many missionaries keep journals, several of which have been published or used as the raw material for biographies and autobiographies.

Concluding thoughts

Spiritual journals are as diverse as the Christians who keep them. However, their common feature is that they provide a record of an individual's journey with God.

For some Christians that pilgrimage is seen almost exclusively in terms of their individual relationship with God. Their journals consequently have little to say about the world in which they live.

For others, particularly those within the evangelical tradition, sacred and secular overlap to a considerable degree. This is because evangelical spirituality at its best insists on seeing the whole of life as a spiritual life. From this perspective, all work is a divine vocation, all play is praise, and our relationship with God is inseparable from our relationships with one another.

For such an inclusive spirituality there is no contradiction between the spiritual journal and other forms of journal keeping. A journey or our observations of the world about us may offer us fresh insights into the goodness of God. In particular the use of the journal as a tool to promote personal growth is not excluded. This is because the biblical concept of salvation is intimately connected with the idea of wholeness. The pilgrimage into God is at the same time a journey towards personal wholeness.

We may expect to find that such a journal reflects the basic movements of the Christian life. First and foremost it will be a record of God's gracious encounter with us and the growth in our capacity to respond in praise. But this is not a solitary existence. The spiritual journal is also a record of our life in the community of the Church and our growth in love for one another. Finally it will record our experience of being directed into the world and our developing response to God's call to service.

A Preliminary Exercise

Begin by finding yourself a place to write. Ideally, it should be a place where you can write in comfort without being disturbed. Set aside a few minutes for the exercise, preferably at a time when you do not have to keep an eye on the clock.

Now relax with pen and paper in front of you. Enjoy the sensation of being able to put your feet up for a few minutes, of being able to stand aside from the rush and pressure of modern life. When you feel ready, consider the following questions.

1. Why are you reading this book? What do you hope or expect to get out of it?

Turn these questions over in your mind for a few minutes. Jot down whatever comes to mind in response to these questions. Your response may be a direct answer or a list of points or a statement that is only loosely related to the questions.

When you have written all that you want to write in response to these questions, you might like to consider the following (either now or at a later date).

2. Does the idea of keeping a journal appeal to you? Is your 'gut reaction' positive or negative?

If it is positive, what specifically attracts you to it?

If your reaction is negative, what are your specific objections? Does it make you feel vulnerable? Are you afraid that someone else might read it? Or do you regard it as a waste of time? If so, why? Is it because you believe your private thoughts and feelings are too trivial to be recorded?

Whatever your reaction remember to jot down your responses to these questions. If you decide to start a journal these notes could be your first entry.

2

Beginning Your Journal

Isn't it obvious how to keep a journal? Surely you can find out by looking at any good desk diary! Imagine it sitting in front of you, waiting to be used. It offers you one page per day (no more and no less) which you must fill with your words of wisdom, observations on life, reflections on God, etc. It clearly expects you to write more or less the same amount every day regardless of time, health, or inspiration.

My experience is that starting a journal without giving some thoughts to the mechanics of it can be a recipe for disappointment. I have lost count of the number of false starts I made as I tried to find a way of keeping a journal which suited my personality and lifestyle. The purpose of this chapter is to warn you of some of the most common pitfalls and to make various suggestions which may help you get off to an enjoyable start.

HARDWARE

Given the incredible range of stationery available nowadays it is all too easy for the would-be journal keeper to begin with materials which do not meet his or her own particular needs.

The notebook

The right notebook is very much a matter of personal preference. However, it is only too easy for our preferences to be overruled by current fashions.

There are two basic requirements which any suitable notebook should meet. The relative importance you place on each will help you decide what type of notebook suits you best. The notebook you choose should be *durable* since your journal may become a lifelong companion. A little extra investment to begin with will more than repay itself by adding years to the life of your notebooks. The notebook should also be *flexible* enough to let you write, or draw, or paste in items from elsewhere. It should not restrict your journal keeping or make you feel that you must write in a particular way. Nor should you feel threatened by it.

Personally, I find hardback pre-printed diaries unhelpful. I feel that they make unreasonable demands and impose unreasonable limits on my journal keeping. They seem to demand an entry every day and, in my experience, this can create a sense of guilt when one fails to make entries regularly. They also restrict the length of journal entries by offering a set space for each day (which may on some occasions be too little and on others too much). I would always choose an undated notebook. On the other hand, some people value the structure that a pre-printed diary brings to their lives. If you are such a person, make sure the diary you choose is large enough for your needs. There is a limit to how much extra paper can be stapled into a hardback book!

The choice of hardback or loose-leaf depends on whether you regard durability or flexibility as more important. For durability a good quality hardback notebook is hard to beat. It is also more compact than the equivalent number of sheets in a loose-leaf binder. Some people find that using a hardback also helps them to resist the temptation to edit their journal (editing is still possible but it remains glaringly obvious). However, hardback notebooks are much less flexible than loose-leaf systems. As with a pre-printed diary, there is a limit to the amount of extra material that can be pasted into the notebook.

For those who regard flexibility as more important, a loose-leaf system is the answer. Using a loose-leaf binder permits you to use blank or ruled paper as required; to use different colours of paper for different purposes; and, to insert letters, magazine articles, newspaper clippings, photographs, pressed flowers, used bus tickets, or whatever takes your fancy, with impunity. However, you must be prepared to cope with a much bulkier journal. Most ring binders are also less durable than a hardback and subject the paper they contain to a good deal of wear and tear. You may need to reinforce the guide holes of the paper you use. This is time consuming and adds to the bulk of the journal. My impression is that the most durable loose-leaf binders are multiple-ring binders (such as Filofax and its clones) and spring-backed binders.

Another factor to consider is the size of your journal. Many journal keepers value portability. They keep their journal handy to record flashes of inspiration as they occur. I know of one or two people who carry A4 notepads around with them but most people prefer something less conspicuous! Of course, it is possible to make notes on the back of an envelope and then transfer them to a master journal kept at home. Personally, I find this too time consuming and I am tempted to edit such entries. Such notes may also be mislaid or lost before you have a chance to transcribe them.

On the other hand, some people find small journals too restrictive. They may be too small to accommodate newspaper cuttings or photographs. Some journal users also find that very small notebooks affect their style of writing, forcing them to write in a way that they feel to be cramped and, perhaps, too cryptic. Another disadvantage of using very small notebooks is that you find yourself starting new volumes at frequent intervals. For many journal keepers, the start of a new volume is a significant occasion, an opportunity to review the previous volume and put their life in perspective. The value of this is considerably reduced if you begin a new volume every month! A small journal may also be a liability when it comes to reviewing: ideally, if it is a hardback, it should be large enough for you to leave a generous margin for subsequent comments.

Finally, if you opt for a hardback notebook, you will have to choose between plain or ruled paper. Experienced journal keepers often recommend plain paper as being more flexible. Blank sheets offer more scope for creativity than ruled sheets (which seem to demand more or less conventional written entries). My own feeling is that, for most of us, creativity is a fragile flower that requires careful nurture. Presenting a newcomer to journal keeping with a blank notebook could be rather like feeding seedlings with concentrated fertiliser! If the prospect of filling a completely blank sheet of paper with whatever you like feels threatening by all means begin with a lined notebook.

After all this advice you may be curious about the type of notebook I use. Over the years I have tried out all the possibilities mentioned above. My own personal compromise is a Filofax system. I can carry current notes with me in a leather binder while old notes are stored in cardboard binders and filing boxes.

Writing instruments

You will want to use a pen or pencil with which you feel comfortable. If you plan to carry the current volume of your journal around with you, it is probably a good idea to make sure that the ink you use is waterproof (particularly if you live in the British Isles!). Since many journal users keep a pen tucked into the pages of their journal another wise precaution is to choose a pen that is not likely to leak.

Ink colour is worth thinking about. Does a particular colour remind you of work or school? If so, you may want to choose some other colour. Or you may wish to experiment with colour coding the contents of your journal: I use blue for general notes, black for quotations and green for dreams.

Alternative to notebooks

Modern technology has created new possibilities for journal keeping. One such is the cassette recorder. Its general availability and ease of use means that keeping a tape journal has become a practical possibility. This is particularly appropriate for those who hate writing or like to think out loud. It also means that those who, for whatever reason, are unable to write are no longer barred from the experience of keeping a journal. Since most of us speak faster than we write, the act of making an entry in a tape journal takes up less time than its more conventional cousin. Nevertheless taped journals do have a number of drawbacks. The most serious is that reviewing such a journal is very time consuming. Another is that tape journals rapidly become very cumbersome. Tapes are also significantly less hard-wearing than notebooks.

Another possibility is the home computer. At the moment most word processing programmes are even more restrictive than a lined notebook (you can ignore the lines in a notebook but that is impossible in a word processor document file). Desk top publishing programmes offer more flexibility: they give you much more control over the layout of text and they allow you to insert graphs, diagrams and other pictures. However, they demand large amounts of memory so individual files may be quite limited in length. Perhaps the most interesting development for potential computer journal keepers is the appearance of much more flexible database programmes. While imposing similar constraints to those of word processed documents, they offer very powerful data retrieval and manipulation facilities.

WHEN SHOULD I MAKE AN ENTRY?

How often?

Should I keep my journal up to date daily? Is a weekly summary sufficient? Can I get away with only writing in the journal when I feel so inclined?

Morton Kelsey advises that entries in a spiritual journal ought to be made daily. This is because the spiritual journal is a record of what ought to be the most important relationship in your life: your relationship with God. Furthermore, he argues, the journal does not merely record but actually stimulates you to go deeper into that relationship. Others

22

argue for daily records because they see the journal as part of a package of spiritual self-discipline.

I agree with the premises of Kelsey's argument but I cannot go along with his conclusions. Why are daily entries the norm for a spiritual journal? If they record the most important relationship in my life should I not make these entries hourly or even more frequently? Any method of journal keeping which insists that entries be made at specific predetermined intervals ignores the fact that the seasons of the soul do not necessarily follow the clock. There is a place for regular entries: they summarise what we have been doing, thinking and experiencing. They anchor special occasions, events and experiences in the context of everyday life.

More important than the regularity of entries is the quality of the time devoted to your journal. Thus my advice about frequency would be: write whenever you feel like it. John Michael Talbot's *Changes: A Spiritual Journal* is a good example of what I mean. Occasionally he makes several entries in a single day. At other times he does not touch his journal for several days or even weeks.

Frequency is also affected by the purpose of your journal. If you regard it as a guide-book to the chief landmarks of your spiritual pilgrimage you may not feel the need to write in it every day. Indeed you may prefer to resort to the practice only on special occasions. Thus you might be led to keep a retreat journal (the spiritual counterpart of the holiday journals mentioned in Chapter 1). My journal is an important companion on retreats (I usually change the colour of my notepaper for such occasions so that they stand out easily).

What time of day?

As with frequency, journal keepers often have strong views about the best time of day for making entries. Some link it with early morning prayer and Bible meditation. However, this should not be taken as a universal rule. For many people, myself included, early morning is by no means their best time of day.

Because I associate journal keeping with the recording of the way God works in my life from day to day, I prefer to make entries in the evening. In the evening, it is possible to review the day in the presence of God.

However the best general advice is that of an American priest, who writes, 'The journal should be kept at a time of day when we are alert, quiet, and capable of coming in tune with our deepest self.'

Dating entries

On the whole, it is a good idea to date entries. You may also find it helpful to note the time of day and (if you travel a lot) where you are. This enables you to put the entries in the context of your personal history as a whole when you come to review your journal. My own experience is that certain undated entries have become virtually meaningless because I can no longer remember the context in which they were written. This is doubly important in a loose-leaf journal where dropping it on the floor could so easily randomise your life history!

WHAT SHOULD I INCLUDE?

Your journal may contain whatever you want to put in it. You are not limited to your own thoughts: you can, for example, include the Bible verse which has just spoken forcibly to you, or any other important quotation. You might like to paste newspaper clippings or important letters into your journal. The content need not even be written: a diary may include photographs, diagrams and sketches. Carl Jung used to summarise his day by drawing mandalas: spontaneous geometric patterns reflecting his feelings about the day.

A journal entry need not be limited to today's events. If something that happened yesterday is on your mind by all means note it down. And the same goes for something that happened last week or ten years ago. Today's memories may be of far greater significance than today's events. It follows that you need never worry about incompleteness. In fact, 'oversights' can often be very illuminating when they occur to you at some later date. Why didn't I make any note of that blazing row with my wife? Why do I never make any reference to X, Y or Z?

PRIVACY AND HONESTY

Privacy

The nearest thing to a rule for keeping a personal journal is that it should be private. By expressing your innermost thoughts and feelings in a journal, you make yourself vulnerable. If you fear that others may read your journal you may write what you believe they would want to read. In extreme cases, such fear may even prevent you from keeping a journal.

Privacy is advisable not only to protect yourself but also to ensure that others are protected too. Your journal may contain comments or observations which could damage your relationship with a potential reader or some third party. In the course of letting off steam in his journal a husband may say some hurtful things about his wife (or vice versa), or a pastor may make cutting remarks about members of his or her congregation.

Honesty

Privacy is a prerequisite for the honesty which makes journal keeping such a valuable exercise. Far from being a form of escapism as some critics suggest, your journal is a haven in which you can safely begin to strip away the illusions with which you hide yourself from others and the delusions with which you hide from yourself. It is a mirror in which you gradually come to see yourself as you really are.

Of course privacy is only the first step to honesty in a journal: the temptation to write what you would like to believe about yourself still remains. Even if you do not actually lie to yourself, you may still launder the truth by omitting events, experiences and feelings that you do not wish to acknowledge as your own. Jim Elliott was very realistic in beginning his journal thus:

> What is written in these pages I suppose will someday be read by others than myself. For this reason I cannot hope to be absolutely honest in what is herein recorded, for the hypocrisy of this shamming heart will ever be putting on a front and dares not to have written what is actually found in its abysmal depths. Yet, I pray, Lord, that You will make these notations to be as nearly true to fact as is possible so that I may know my own

heart and be able to definitely pray regarding my gross, though often unviewed, inconsistencies.[1]

I think Jim Elliott hit upon a key to honesty in the context of a spiritual journal. While we delude ourselves only too easily, there is no deluding God. This and the realisation that the God who loves us places a very high value on honesty set us free to be ourselves before God.

Consciously bringing God as a partner into the process of keeping a journal, is to offer him the perfect opportunity to destroy our self-delusion. But how can we know whether we are being honest with ourselves and God? Self-delusion is notoriously hard to recognise. We 'honestly' imagine ourselves to be more spiritual than we really are. The Pharisee in Jesus' parable of the Pharisee and the tax collector is typical. He approached God secure in the belief that he was spiritually mature and doing what was pleasing to God. In fact, he was spiritually complacent. On the other hand, the example of the tax collector suggests a way of recognising when we are being honest with ourselves and God. He approached God in sheer terror. That is an extreme case, but if our writing makes us feel vulnerable then we are probably succeeding in stripping away the masks behind which we hide from God, our fellows and ourselves.

Ways and means

What steps can be taken to ensure the privacy of your journal? You could follow the example of Beatrix Potter and write in code. With practice it is possible to become quite fluent and it has the advan-

1. *The Journals of Jim Elliott*, p. 11.

27

tage of being completely secure against casual readers. However, it has one major disadvantage: Beatrix Potter allowed her journal to lapse and when she returned to it in later life she discovered that she had forgotten the key. It wasn't until some years after her death that the notebooks were finally deciphered.

For most people anonymity will probably be sufficient protection. A journal is more likely to be read if you emblazon its cover with 'My private journal. Do not read!' and leave it lying on your desk. Ostentatious journal keeping often indicates a desire (conscious or subconscious) to have someone read it. If you feel that the anonymity of unmarked notebooks kept in a drawer is insufficient, you may want to lock them away in a cupboard or suitcase.

A useful technique for protecting those you write about is to use initials or nicknames or both. I know someone who refers to her children as RS (reluctant scholar) and IBG (I'm a big girl now).

You may wish to take extra precautions if your journal is portable. If it is loose-leaf the bulk can remain safely at home with just the current page and some spare paper in a portable binder. A hardback journal could be given a third party address so that, if it were lost, it might eventually find its way back without your identity becoming known. Ira Progoff organises such a system for American users of his Intensive Journal method. British users might wish to make arrangements for the journal to be returned through a trusted friend, their minister, or a P.O. box.

Many people are put off journal keeping by the belief that you need to be able to write 'good English'. School has taught them that correct spelling, punctuation and grammar are essential prerequisites of all writing. This would be true if they were planning to write a book. However, since the journal is not a book, the usual constraints do not apply. All that matters is that *you* can understand what you have written.

Of course, if 'good English' and the visual impact of the written page are important to you by all means pay attention to them. A friend of mine regards her journal very much as a creative activity. She takes great care with each entry, sometimes writing them in verse and including illustrations.

Another aspect of style is the length of entries. At one extreme you might have the leisure and inclination to fill your journal with extended essays. The opposite extreme is a technique known as headlining: summarising your day in a single pithy statement, a newspaper headline. Either of these extremes, and everything in between, is quite legitimate in your journal.

While on the subject of style, I have one word of advice on editing: don't! You may be tempted to edit for a variety of reasons. What you have written may seem trivial to you and not worthy of the space it takes up. However, that may be because of your present mood. Such an entry may speak forcibly to you in years to come. It may be that on rereading you discover statements with which you can no longer agree. If so, it is better to add a dated comment to that effect than to delete the offending lines. After all, you did believe them at one time. Even something as apparently random as spelling mistakes may strike you as significant at a later date.

These are not rules but merely a collection of hints and suggestions gleaned from experienced journal keepers.

Spontaneity

'Write fast, write everything, include everything, write from your feelings, write from your body, accept whatever comes.'[2] Following this advice will help you nurture a spontaneous approach to journal keeping which is a valuable aid to honest writing. Most of us tend to sit in judgement on what we say or write. Writing as fast as possible may enable you to disable this internal censor sufficiently to permit the real you to be reflected in the pages of your journal.

This is not to be confused with automatic writing (advocated by the surrealist school of art) which involves the deliberate suppression of normal mental processes in an attempt to permit the subconscious to express itself freely. It is closely related to occult techniques which seek to allow external psychic forces to express themselves. Such wilful abandonment of yourself to possession by forces over which you have no control has no place in a journal kept as part of a Christian spiritual discipline.

2. Tristine Rainer, *The New Diary*, p. 34.

Writing for an audience

You may find that, in spite of all your security precautions, you still write as if you were addressing an audience. If so, you may turn this to your advantage by consciously choosing that audience. At the same time, you must recognise that your choice will significantly affect the content of your journal. For example, what you might say to your children will differ from what you might say to your parents.

The example of Jim Elliott suggests that a spiritual journal might be addressed to God. Subsequent reviews of such journals can be very revealing about what aspects of your life you regard as relevant to God.

Multiple journals?

The possibility of different audiences raises the possibility of keeping different journals for different purposes. For example, you might want to keep a spiritual journal, a private secular journal, a dream journal, a family journal and a professional journal. Ira Progoff's *Intensive Journal* may be regarded as an example of this approach. He divides the journal into several parallel sections dealing with different aspects of your life.

At the other extreme, Tristine Rainer advocates a single chronological journal in which all these aspects mix together. In this way, the journal reflects the unity to which she aspires in her daily life. Her approach is simpler and avoids difficulties over where to put a particular entry. Futhermore, the ideal of unity of purpose is one which has been shared by many Christians. Journal keeping can encourage this unity by forcing me to interrelate different aspects of my life.

However, experience has taught me that a single all-encompassing journal may not be a practical possibility. I keep two journals: a chronological private journal and a more systematic professional one. This is not, as Rainer suggests, a symptom of my failure to relate my work to my private life. It is merely a necessity forced on me by the sheer volume of the notes associated with my work!

A miscellany of techniques

The range of possibilities is endless. I shall deal with many of them in subsequent chapters but here is a brief summary to whet your appetite.

Lists. All of us make lists: shopping lists, lists of things we must do, letters we must write, lists of resolutions, books to read, etc. They are so much a part of modern life that we often don't think of them as also being an integral part of a journal. In fact, their usefulness extends far beyond merely listing things to do or buy. They can be used to summarise experiences, feelings, beliefs, etc. In the context of a spiritual journal they might appear in the form of prayer lists. Many journal keepers regard them as valuable time and space savers. They are also very helpful in putting problems into perspective and organising our response to those problems.

Unsent letters are another common type of journal entry. They may be used to express what you really feel about some person or situation. As I shall explain later, I also use them as a form of prayer.

Dialogues are an imaginative way of reflecting on your relationships with anyone or anything. Journal keepers have used them to examine their personal relationships, God, aspects of their personality, their feelings about their body, human institutions, their work. Together with lists, they form the backbone of Ira Progoff's *Intensive Journal* method.

Written daydreams. In the pages of your journal you can record your dreams, expand on half-remembered dream fragments, daydream about the subject of your choice. Closely related to this is the use of imagination in Bible reading and meditation.

Diagrams and pictures. Sometimes words cannot express just what you want to say. If you feel so inclined, you can use the pages of your journal to give pictorial expression to your experiences and feelings. For non-artists like me the privacy of the journal keeps such doodling safe from the critical eyes of others.

CONCLUSION: THE 'NO RULE' RULE

If I had to summarise the content of this chapter in one sentence it would be, 'There are no rules'. The suggestions I have made are meant to stimulate you to create your own methods of keeping a journal. They are not a set of rules to which you must conform.

After all, your journal is unique to you. Just as its form and content are relevant to you alone so the precise balance of techniques you adopt will be unique.

Exercises

You may feel that you simply want to get on with writing in your journal. If so, that's fine. On the other hand you may want some specific exercise as a way to get started. In that case you might like to try one or more of the following.

As with the exercise at the end of chapter 1, it is a good idea to set aside sufficient time to relax and tackle the exercise in a leisurely manner.

(i) Soul map

Take a full page in your journal to draw a map of an imaginary country which represents the state of your soul. Spend some time filling in the topographical details. Give them specific names, e.g., 'the desert of loneliness at work'.

When it is complete, take a good look at it. How do you feel about this representation of your soul? Can you summarise your feelings in a single phrase or sentence? Is there any aspect of the map that you particularly like or dislike? Have you omitted anything? Write out your reactions, feelings and reflections.

(ii) My personal creed

This is a listing exercise. At the top of a new page write, 'I believe in . . .'. Now list the first ten things that come into your head. Take time to reflect on one or more of these beliefs. Where did you come by the belief? Did it come from your parents? Friends? Reading? School? Church? Why do you believe it? What difference does it make to your life? Try to be specific as you write your responses.

This exercise could be repeated with such statements as, 'I do not believe in . . .' or 'I no longer believe in . . .'.

(iii) What time is it in my life?

Take a few minutes to consider this question. When you are ready draw a clock face at the top of a sheet of paper. Mark on the clock face the time of day which most closely reflects where you are in your life. Write about your answer to this question. What are your feelings about this time? What are its positive and negative implications for your life?

Alternatively, you could proceed by means of another listing exercise. Make lists with the following headings, 'It is too late for . . .', 'It is too early for . . .', 'It is the right time for . . .', 'I need time for . . .'.

3

The Journal and Prayer

As you might expect, prayer is a recurring theme of spiritual journals. It finds its way into journals in a number of different ways, some obvious, others less so.

Perhaps the most obvious way is the tendency for Christians to refer to the content of their intercessions in their journals. The habit of recording your prayers, of keeping a prayer journal, is a good one to develop. Such prayer journals may be kept by individuals or members of a regular prayer meeting. For example, at Little Gidding we maintain an intercession book for use in the Community's daily prayers.

One method is to divide a page in your journal into two columns. In one column you keep your prayer record. The other column is left blank: to be filled in later as you discern answers to your prayers.

Jim Elliott makes a comment that neatly summarises the main advantage of keeping such a record: 'It is not written as a diary of my experiences or feelings but more as a "book of remembrance" to enable me to ask definitely by forcing myself to put yearnings into words.'[1] The attempt to write down your prayers (even in summary form) will make it glaringly obvious to you whether they are definite

1. *The Journals of Jim Elliott*, p. 83.

requests or vague yearnings. Not only does such recording make you conscious of vagueness in prayer but it actually encourages you to reformulate your intercessions in a more specific form.

Another major advantage of keeping a prayer record lies in that blank column kept for answers to prayer. It encourages you to expect answers. With the passage of time it enables you to discern God's involvement in your life and in the world around you. Just as important as this personal confirmation of faith in God's providential care is the fact that this record provides you with a concrete basis for personal thanksgiving.

However, the relevance of journal keeping to prayer is by no means limited to recording your intercessions. A spiritual journal may refer to any and every aspect of prayer (and worship). Jim Elliott's journal is a good contemporary example.

It is worth making particular mention of the use of the journal as a place for self-examination and confession. The idea of sacramental confession before a priest seems alien to many Christians and the old tradition of public confession before the local congregation (the penitents' pew) has long since disappeared from our churches. And yet people still feel a real need to confess their sins to God.

For many people, that need is met by keeping a journal. Indeed, the use of journals as confessionals is so important that Thomas Mallon devotes an entire chapter to 'Confessors' in his fascinating study of published diaries, *A Book of One's Own*. Similarly, Tristine Rainer speaks of an entire category of journal writing which she calls *cathartic* writing. Because of its importance, I shall devote much of chapter 5 to this topic.

Although many Christians write about their prayer lives in their journals, far fewer go on to pray in the pages of those journals. Why is this?

Part of the reason may be a suspicion of written prayers. There are certainly some people who question whether written prayers are genuine. They may feel that the practice of writing prayers is too cold and formal. Others may feel that they have so much to say to God that there just isn't time to write it all down. Or they may feel that the rules of grammar prevent them from saying on paper precisely what they want to say. I believe that such fears are unfounded. They arise, in part, from the false impression created by traditional education that there is a 'correct' way of writing. As we have already seen, such rules are only important if you are writing for public consumption.

It is worth noting that the Hebrews had no such hang-ups about written prayers. This is seen most clearly in the Book of Psalms. There we have a body of prayers which have been reused in public and private worship for millennia. Similarly the writers of the New Testament were quite happy to record prayers when it seemed right to do so.

What is prayer?

An important factor in determining whether you feel that written prayers are appropriate will be your understanding of prayer itself. Some approaches to prayer sit more easily with the written word than others.

It is possible to classify approaches to prayer into four broad groups. The most primitive kind of prayer is *manipulative* prayer. Motivated by fear, superstition or self-interest, this approach consists of techniques which are intended to enable the practitioner to gain his or her own ends by manipulating the spiritual dimension of reality. Amongst those techniques would be found the writing of manipulative prayers (or magical incantations). Such prayer is by no means limited to the so-called primitive religions or to occultism. The tele-evangelist who asks you to write out your request and place it on top of the set while he prays is encouraging precisely this approach. The psychoanalyst who commends prayer as a technique for achieving personal well-being is tending in this direction. So too is the preacher who draws too close a connection between right ways of praying and material success.

The classical reaction against this spiritual manipulation has sometimes been called *philosophical* prayer. This reminds us of the Greek philosophical tradition which by and large rejected the former approach with its rather low view of God. Instead they encouraged an approach to prayer as simple acceptance of the way the world is. Such (thankful) resignation in the face of reality found its way into Christianity and still appears to this day in one form or another. As far as the value of written prayer is concerned, such an approach tends to encourage a passivity which makes speaking or writing equally inappropriate.

A third approach to prayer which is quite widespread within the Christian churches is that of *mystical* prayer. Here the emphasis is on contemplation of the Infinite. In non-Christian forms God may be regarded as an impersonal cosmic force and contemplation becomes attuning yourself to the universe. In Christianity it becomes a quest for a stillness of heart and mind in the presence of the living God. It is an expression of desire for the life that will only fully be realised in the Kingdom of God. As such it has a proper part to play in Christian spirituality. However, it can become rather élitist. Those who fall into this trap may dismiss spoken (and, by extension, written) prayer as inferior and only suitable for spiritual beginners.

The fourth approach is what the German theologian Friedrich Heiler has called *prophetic* prayer. This is characteristic of (if not unique to) the biblical religions. It is based upon the belief that God is supremely personal and that he is intimately involved in the life of this world, caring for every conceivable level of existence. Here prayer becomes a dialogue between God and human beings. When we pray in this way we do two things: we express our response to the love of God and we align ourselves with the will of God. Thus it embraces thanksgiving and praise, but also confessions, petitions, complaints, questions, and expressions of doubt. Above all, it is prayer which expects a response.

Clearly this fourth approach to prayer is at the heart of every Christian spiritual tradition. Since it regards prayer as dialogue, spoken prayer has often played an essential role in this approach. However, it is by no means limited to *spoken* dialogues. What matters is the fact that prayer is a dialogue, not that it is spoken. It is equally possible to have a dialogue by means of the written word.

How can written prayers help?

There is nothing in the Christian understanding of prayer which would rule out the use of your journal as a medium for prayer. But are there positive reasons in favour of written prayers? I believe that written prayer is a valuable practice and I have found that it has helped me in the following ways.

For me, this form of prayer has really come into its own at times when I have found spoken prayer difficult. For example, I find writing letters to God an invaluable aid to concentration when I am too tired or distracted to be able to pray normally (when I am too tired to concentrate on writing to God, I know it is time to go to bed!).

Even when I am not tired, I find that praying on paper forces me to pay more attention to my prayers. I find it only too easy to hurry through spoken prayers when I am busy; to fire a few sentences at God as I rush on to the next thing I have to do, and to fool myself that this is prayer. Writing my prayers slows me down and forces me to concentrate more wholeheartedly on the whole procedure.

Writing down your prayers also makes them more accessible for the purpose of self-examination. Without such a record it is far easier to have a general impression that your prayer life is fine. C. S. Lewis once commented that it is very easy for imaginative people to believe that their spiritual state is much more advanced than is in fact the case. Praying in your journal is a very effective way of pricking that particular bubble.

A record of your prayer times enables you to take a self-critical look at this aspect of your life. It can help you become more aware of how you speak to God. As with the recording of intercessions, it forces us to be more specific and warns us if we are slipping into vague generalities. Our use of standard formulae and religious clichés becomes glaringly obvious when we start to write down our prayers. It may even have things to teach us about our understanding of our relationship with God. For example, does the form of address and the style of the prayer suggest that you regard God as an intimate friend, or an awesome monarch, or both at the same time? Or does it reveal that you have been slipping into a manipulative form of prayer?

LETTERS TO GOD

The most obvious approach to praying in your journal is simply to write down what you would normally have spoken (either aloud or in your head). However, you may feel self-conscious about doing this. If so, you might find it helpful to try a technique which I have been using for some years: I write letters to God. The idea first came to me when I read Morris West's novel *The Clowns of God* (in which a runaway pope writes open letters to God as a way of publicising his views). Perhaps I should add that I regard written prayers as a useful supplement to spoken prayer rather than a permanent substitute.

Letter writing is a common strategy of journal keepers. George Simons says of the technique, 'Such letters in the journal, even when addressed to actual persons, are not written with the intention of being sent. They are rather devices to aid us in searching out and freeing our actual thoughts and feelings.'[2] What I am suggesting is rather different. While I agree that such unsent letters can be valuable journal exercises, I believe that you can write actual letters to God in the pages of your journal. The act of writing is itself an act of prayer.

2. George Simons, *Keeping Your Personal Journal*, p. 63.

Preparation

Since it is an act of prayer, it is worth spending a little time beforehand in order to achieve an appropriate attitude. Just like communication in a love relationship between two humans, prayer benefits from being relaxed and unhurried. One step towards achieving this sort of atmosphere is simply to choose an appropriate time of day. Another very important step is to make a conscious effort to relax. Surprisingly few Christians take such preparation seriously. Too often we try to pray while we are still tense and distracted by all the burdens and anxieties of the day.

Because it is so important, both to prayer in general and to the practice of keeping a spiritual journal, here are some suggestions about how you might relax and turn your attention to God before beginning to pray (or write).

(a) Focus on *breathing*: take up your prayer (or writing) position. Now relax, beginning with the muscles of your face (particularly around your eyes and jaw). Are they tense? Consciously release the tension. If you are not sure, try deliberately tensing the muscles and releasing them. Move progressively down through your neck, shoulders, chest, stomach, arms and hands, legs and feet.

Observe your breathing (don't change it, yet!). Is it smooth? If not, slowly even it out. Is it deep? If not, gradually deepen it. Is it rapid? If so, gradually slow it down.

Close your eyes and establish a pattern of slow, deep, even breathing. Allow a mood of inner concentration gradually to set in.

(b) Focus on *listening*: consciously relax your muscles, as before.

Close your eyes and listen to the sounds around you. Sounds only distract us when we try to fight them. Instead, let the sounds penetrate your being. Accept them and wait for a mood of quiet to set in.

(c) Focus on *sensation*: relax your body. Become aware of your clothes gripping your shoulders, arms, legs; your shoes touching your feet; the sensation of the chair against your body; the movement of the air around you. Monitor these sensations until you begin to experience an inner relaxation.

Whatever method you choose, the key step in the process of preparing to pray is to open yourself to God's presence. A simple prayer asking God for his help in this process is appropriate. Some people like to use the Jesus Prayer ('Lord Jesus Christ, Son of the living God, have mercy on me, a sinner'), repeating it in conjunction with their breathing. Others may prefer to base their prayer on an appropriate verse of Scripture, e.g., 'Pause a while and know that I am God' (Ps. 46:10).

The letter itself

'Isn't letter writing too formal to express the intimacy of prayer?' My reply to that objection would be, 'What about love letters?'

A letter to God is best thought of as a love letter. Indeed the very intimate context, i.e., your personal journal (the place where you are free to reveal the real you), requires that any genuine letters be addressed only to those with whom you are closest.

Perhaps I should explain what I understand by a love letter. I do not mean pages of 'sweet nothings'. A love letter can be informative and descriptive; it can contain specific information and requests. It can even contain complaints and angry words. It can contain what any other letter can contain because what makes it distinctive is not its content but its motivation. A love letter is an act of self-giving. It is a pouring out of your news, your thoughts, your feelings; it is a pouring out of yourself. Clearly such a letter calls for a degree of honesty similar to that which would be normal in a journal.

One way of beginning to write prayer letters to God is simply to put into your letters the things you would normally have shared with him in spoken prayer. Alternatively, you might like to devote your letter to a specific topic or problem (see exercise 2 at the end of the chapter). This is particularly appropriate if you regard such written prayers as an occasional supplement to other methods. Perhaps you might use letter writing as a way of tackling particularly important or difficult issues.

A third approach would be to turn your normal journal entries into letters or written prayers. In this way you would be bringing before God all the aspects of your life which you regarded as significant. An extension of this approach would be to address the entire journal to God. In a sense it can become a single unending letter to God. While not strictly a journal, St Augustine's *Confessions* is a good example of a piece of writing addressed to God. If you opt for this approach, you may still find it helpful to write letters to God from time to time. It is only too easy to start out with the intention of writing your journal for God and to slip into writing it for yourself or some other audience. Occasional letters to God will serve to remind you of your commitment to write the whole thing for him to read.

Conclusion

When you have finished your letter you have not finished praying. If I am right in regarding dialogue with God as central to the Christian understanding of prayer, then prayer is only completed by God's response. We cannot compel God to respond to our prayers (whether spoken or written) but we can express our willingness to listen for his response and to act upon it.

One way of expressing such willingness is to spend a minute or two in silence at the end of each prayer time. This is time spent simply waiting for God to speak. Keep your journal handy to record any thoughts or insights which occur to you then. However, don't simply assume that such thoughts must be the voice of God. They might be nothing more than the voice of your own imagination (that is why the Bible warns us to test the spirits: all such insights must be checked against the teaching of Scripture).

If nothing comes to you, don't worry. God is not limited by the amount of time you can devote to listening for a reply. You may find that the next time you read the Bible, or listen to a sermon, or talk to a friend, or turn on the television something strikes you with the force of a revelation. Or the response may be a definite answer to your prayers. Anything is possible with God. If you keep your journal with you, you will be well placed to record and test anything which appears to be a divine response.

THE JOURNAL AS AN AID TO WORSHIP

Can the journal be of any use in private worship? Worship is essentially the expression of your joy in the Lord. Such an outpouring of joy is the very

46

antithesis of words such as cool, logical, sensible, balanced. One of the most important things that charismatic renewal has to teach us is that there is nothing careful or premeditated about praise and worship. Thanks to that movement we have greater freedom today to express our joy.

In the light of such an experience of praise, one that transcends the usual limits of human language, is there any place for journal keeping? Can something as word-centred as a journal be of any value in contemporary praise?

I believe that journal keeping can have a role here. It is a mistake to think that we no longer need words which have been strung together in a way that makes sense.The nonrational praise of speaking (or singing) in tongues and the silence of contemplative prayer together liberate praise from the stranglehold of the articulate and the educated. The public expression of praise is no longer the exclusive preserve of the few. But we are still rational creatures, called to love the Lord with all our minds.

A major role of the journal as an aid to worship is in capturing the little moments of joy in each day. The journal is an ideal place for recording and experiencing afresh the positive, the creative, and the life-enhancing aspects of your daily life. St Paul advised us to 'fill your minds with everything that is true, everything that is noble, everything that is good and pure, everything that we love and honour, and everything that can be thought virtuous or worthy of praise' (Phil. 4:8). This is much more than an exhortation to meditate on the Scriptures (though it is that as well). It is a call to focus on all that is good and positive in our culture and in our day-to-day experience. Recording those things in a journal is one way of doing that.

This is a valuable exercise even at a purely secular level. Tristine Rainer devotes an entire chapter of her book, *The New Diary*, to using a journal as a way of discovering joy. Perhaps the best known example of a journal used in this way is Annie Dillard's prize-winning *Pilgrim at Tinker Creek*. She not only records moments of joy experienced during her year in the Blue Ridge Mountains but she also evokes joy in her experience of the natural cycles of life and death in that place. Not all of those experiences are pleasurable; joy is by no means identical with pleasure.

Joy is intensity of experience rather than a pleasant experience. Translated into religious terms, it is our experience of the numinous: those moments in which you become aware of God's presence brooding in and above creation. It is what made the psalmist say,

> I look up at your heavens, made by your fingers,
> at the moon and stars you set in place –
> ah, what is man that you should spare a thought
> for him,
> the son of man that you should care for him?
>
> (Ps. 8:3f)

You *can* capture such moments in words. They may not mean much to anyone else but even a brief record of the experience can be enough to recapture it for you.

Exercises

(i) Begin an intercessions list

As I suggested above the mechanics of this is straightforward. All you need to do is take a page in your journal and divide it with a vertical line (perhaps allowing about two-thirds of the page for notes about your intercessions and the remainder to record your perceptions of God's answers to your prayers).

One of the things which causes people to give up this sort of discipline is simply that they try to concern themselves with too many things. Effective prayer is prayer that is focussed on the matters that really concern you. A prayer list in your journal can help you focus on those major concerns if you are selective in what you include.

Here is one possible way of beginning such a selective prayer list.

Begin by relaxing (perhaps using one of the methods mentioned in the chapter). After a few minutes, ask God to guide you as you think about the matters for which you should be praying. As things occur to you note them down until you have a list of perhaps ten or twelve items. To begin with, this is probably as many items as you can handle. Don't worry about 'mistakes', you can always modify the list in the light of your experience of praying through the items on it.

If you like, you can organise this list in the form of a personalised daily prayer cycle, praying for one or two items on a specific day each week. And you could organise these items thematically (e.g., praying for your church one day, your family another day, and so on).

(ii) A letter to God

Here is one way of using a letter to God as an occasional prayer exercise.

As usual, spend a few minutes relaxing before you begin to pray. When you are relaxed make a list of four or five things which are on your mind at the moment. Look over that list before God. Does any one item strike you as particularly important, or problematic, or difficult? Or is there a particular cause of thanksgiving or joy?

Tell God about it in your letter. Use the letter as a vehicle to express your real feelings about whatever you have chosen to write about. Do you have any thoughts about the subject? Share those as well.

When you have finished your letter, spend a few minutes in silence. Note down anything that occurs to you. Does any action suggest itself to you?

(iii) Count your blessings

In this exercise you follow the same listing procedure as before. However, this time the subject matter is your day (or the past week, or some other appropriate period of time).

After relaxing and becoming aware of God's presence, begin to list all the things for which you can give thanks in the period of time you are considering. The act of making the list is itself an act of thanksgiving but you may want to supplement each item with spoken or unspoken thanks.

(iv) Titles of God

The purpose of this exercise is to expand your perception of God as an aid to worship.

Begin by relaxing. As you become aware of God's

presence, consider the ways in which he makes an impact on your life. Draw on your personal experience of God's activity to prepare a list of names or titles for God.

Unlike most listing exercises, there is no upper limit to this one. Just keep going until you have exhausted the possibilities that occur to you.

Now look over the list again. Do any particular names or titles stand out? Have any fresh insights into God occurred to you during this exercise? Use your responses as the basis for a period of worship.

4

Developing a Christian Imagination

Christianity has a strong intellectual tradition which
is reflected in recurrent calls for Christians to
develop a Christian mind. As a theologian I would
heartily endorse such reminders that we are to love
God with our minds. However, that is only one
dimension of our calling as Christians: 'you must
love the Lord your God with all your heart, with all
your soul, with all your mind and with all your
strength' (Mark 12:30). When Jesus issued that
revision of the Great Commandment he meant it to
be taken as a call to devote *every* aspect of your life
to God.

Indeed that commandment might be taken as a
definition of Christian spirituality. Christianity as a
way of life (as opposed to an institution or a cultural
artefact) is total devotion to the God who has
revealed himself in Jesus. The Danish philosopher
and journal writer Kierkegaard used to say, 'Purity
of heart is to will one thing.' In a Christian context,
such willing can only mean actively directing every
aspect of your life towards God.

In this chapter I want to highlight another area of
life which is often neglected by Christians, namely,
the imagination. My reason for doing so is twofold.
It is particularly relevant in the present context
because keeping a spiritual journal is an excellent
way of developing a Christian imagination. How-

ever, I also believe that the imagination is a vitally important dimension of the human psyche. At the end of a century in which so much research has been done on the nonrational aspects of human psychology we cannot pretend to be unaware of the great power of the human imagination.

But if the imagination is so important why have Christians neglected it for so long? One reason is that, in the history of spirituality, imagination has often been seen in a negative light. We may be most conscious of our imagination at the most inopportune times. It is an important source of the distractions and temptations which bubble up within us whenever we attempt to pray or worship God. Another part of the explanation is that, as western Christians, we are part of a culture which has notoriously neglected the nonrational dimensions of the psyche.

There is also a less worthy motive behind the neglect. The creativity of the human imagination is one of the wellsprings of human freedom. As such, imagination is a threat to all who wish to impose their authority on others. In this connection, there is a significant contrast between the attitude to dreams which held sway in the early church and that of mediaeval catholicism. The former regarded dreams as potentially revelatory while the latter denounced such a view of dreams. A reason is not hard to find: if God could speak directly to a peasant girl, that would detract from the power of the ecclesiastical hierarchy.

THE BIBLE AND YOUR JOURNAL

Ever since Christians began to keep personal journals, notes about their meditation on Scripture have found a home there. Such notes can be found in journals written by Christians of all traditions but they are a particular characteristic of evangelical journals.

A distinction does need to be drawn between recording notes about your Bible reading in your journal and keeping a chronological record of your Bible study. While the latter is a perfectly legitimate practice it is not appropriate within the pages of a personal journal. It is only too easy for a journal to be completely swamped by Bible study notes. If this happens, it may be a useful chronological commentary on your Bible reading but it is no longer a personal journal.

Evangelicals in particular need to be ruthless about what Bible study notes they record in their journals. The journal is about you, not about the many interesting things you find in your reading. So what is appropriate to record? I would recommend that you include only those insights from Scripture which are of particular personal importance. For example, if on reading, 'Do not harness yourself in an uneven team with unbelievers' (2 Cor. 6:14), you are overwhelmed with the sense that you should terminate a particular relationship, that would be a legitimate journal entry. If, on the other hand, it came merely as a theoretical insight that certain kinds of relationship between believers and unbelievers are inappropriate, that might better be recorded in a separate Bible study notebook.

The distinction between a Bible study notebook and a journal lies in the greater personal emphasis of the latter. The journal is the place for recording anything which is of particular personal importance.

This is not the place to go into details about the mechanics of Bible study. However, I would like to

54

look briefly at the art of meditative reading because it can act as a useful bridge between purely intellectual Bible study and more imaginative uses of the Bible. This *lectio divina* as it is sometimes called was originally developed by St Benedict as a way of reading the Bible. Since then it has been found to be helpful by Christians of all traditions. Today it is recommended by both Roman Catholic writers such as Anthony de Mello and Margaret Hebblethwaite and evangelicals such as Richard Foster and Campbell McAlpine. It is also applicable to virtually any kind of book.

Essentially *lectio divina* is prayerful reading. It begins with relaxation and prayer (the techniques for preparation mentioned in the last chapter would be equally applicable here). Once you are still and waiting in the presence of God you begin to read *slowly*. As you read, take time to pause and ponder over individual words and phrases which seem particularly meaningful to you. In focussing on a particular word, feel free to make use of *all* your psychological functions. By all means think about its meaning but remember that meditative reading is more than intellectual study. If appropriate, try to picture what you are reading about. Consider your feelings about the word or phrase: why did you stop here? Do you feel awe, joy, guilt? Apply your intuition: what associations does the word or phrase give rise to?

But the most important stage of *lectio divina* is turning all of this thinking, feeling, sensing and intuition into prayer. Using what you have been reading as the basis of prayer is the key part of meditative reading. It is far more important than writing down any insights you might have.

Finally, when you have pondered and prayed,

take a few minutes to review your prayer time. It is at this point that your journal is useful. Make brief notes about how the time has been; any important personal insights; your feelings, etc.

I hope it is clear from my description of meditative reading that one of its chief enemies is haste. Such an approach to Scripture is completely undermined if you attempt it in conjunction with a Bible reading programme which demands that you get through so many books in a year. Such programmes have their place but not in this context. Meditative reading is not concerned with getting through so many pages a day. It is concerned with allowing God to speak to you through the written word. If you find that the same passage is a source of fresh insight for days or even weeks, don't worry. Let your pace be dictated by what you are getting out of it and not by some external plan or lectionary.

There is a still more imaginative use of the Bible which can be modified easily for use in conjunction with a journal. This is the method developed by Ignatius Loyola in his *Spiritual Exercises*. It is particularly appropriate as a way of reading story passages from the Bible, using your imagination to enter into the flow of the story and thus relive it.

By using your imagination you can become a participant in the events described in the Bible. For example, you can imagine yourself to be part of the crowd listening to Jesus, or you can become one of the characters in the story. As you relive the story, consider what you are experiencing; what you are feeling; how such an experience might change your life or affect your relationships. In some cases it might be appropriate to use such a reliving of a biblical passage as the basis for entering into a conversation with Jesus. And all of this can take place entirely in your head or on the pages of a journal. I find it helpful to use a journal because the act of writing helps to keep me focussed on the scene I am trying to imagine. Examples of this type of exercise can be found in the practical suggestions at the end of the chapter.

WORKING WITH YOUR DREAMS

One point at which even the most unimaginative person comes face to face with the power of his or her imagination is in dreams. That they are closely connected to imagination is not in doubt but beyond that, there is no consensus about the nature of dreams, their function or their value to us.

At one extreme is the outright rejection of dreams by those who place a very high value on consciousness and rationality. For example, the Nobel prize-winning biochemist Francis Crick dismisses dreaming as the dustbin of the brain. Similar sentiments may be found in the writings of the pioneer experimental psychologist Wilhelm Wundt, who regarded dreams as a type of illusion, and in the founder of western philosophy, Plato, who believed them to be the expression of the beast in man.

However, such a dismissive view of dreams is, in my view, completely undermined by the well-documented value of certain dreams. One example will suffice to demonstrate the usefulness of dreams: that of the chemist Friedrich Kekulé. In 1865 he was struggling with the chemical structure of benzene. One day he fell asleep on a bus and as he slept he dreamt. In the course of that dream he imagined snakes chasing their tails. One of the snakes became a spinning ring of carbon atoms: the correct answer to the problem he had been working on!

A more positive view of dreams has been established this century by the development of psychoanalysis. The pioneer in this was Sigmund Freud. However, he regarded dreams as largely pathological, revealing in symbolic form that which the conscious personality had repressed. This interest in dreams was taken up and developed much further by Carl Jung, who regarded dreams as an important way of gaining access to the unconscious dimensions of the human mind.

Dreams are also a recurring theme in the Bible. This is hardly surprising when you consider that most people in biblical times regarded dreams as divinely inspired messages or prophecies (Plato's view, mentioned above, was by no means representative of the average Greek of his day).

But what does the Bible have to say about dreams? The most striking thing is that, compared with the Babylonians and Egyptians, the Hebrews were quite matter of fact about dreams. The author of Ecclesiastes recognised that dreams could simply be the result of our anxieties (Eccles. 5:3) and the prophet Jeremiah warns against false prophets whose dreams are nothing more than the products of their own minds (Jer. 23:25f). Unlike their neighbours, the Hebrews did not believe that dreams were necessarily divine. On the other hand, they were equally clear that dreams could be the medium by which God chose to speak to us. There is a clear connection between dreams, visions and prophecies (Joel 2:28). The New Testament has little to add to this view of dreams. What it does is endorse this view (Acts 2:17) and offer one or two examples of visions or dreams which significantly affected the mission of the early church (Acts 10:10ff, 16:9).

Clearly dreams can take many different forms.

Some are pure fantasy while others seem to be replaying or anticipating everyday events. My own experience suggests that the latter are more common when external events are making great demands upon us, e.g., when I was a student I often had dreams about exams (surprisingly they were by no means all nightmares!). As for the pure fantasies, Morton Kelsey advises that we treat such dreams as referring to our own lives rather than to the lives of others.

Fantasy dreams are of particular interest to psychoanalysts because they are such rich sources of symbols drawn from the deepest layers of the unconscious (the so-called collective unconscious). Such symbols find their way into human culture through our myths and rituals. Interestingly the symbolic element in Kekulé's dream, the snake chasing its tail, is well-known in mythology and alchemy.

One type of dream which is particularly relevant in the present context is the numinous dream. By this I mean a dream in which you experience a sense of awe or religious ecstasy. Morton Kelsey makes the following comment about such dream experiences: 'When a great experience is given in a dream, it is our natural inclination simply to bask in it. One should at least write poetry or a story about the experience.'[1]

What are we to make of dreams and what have they to do with the practice of keeping a personal journal? I think the biblical approach to dreams is fundamentally sound. Dreams are an interesting and potentially valuable phenomenon through which God can speak if he so chooses. If that is the case then our dreams are worth recording.

1. *Adventure Inwards*, p. 119.

This is the point at which the journal becomes invaluable. Most dreams simply evaporate if they are not immediately recorded. If you keep your journal by your bedside then you can make brief notes about any dreams you recall on waking.

Someone may say, 'I never dream'. Most psychologists today would regard that as very unlikely. It is more likely that you simply do not remember dreaming. Often, you will find that the mere decision to keep a record of your dreams is sufficient to evoke their recollection. If this does not have the desired effect, take a critical look at your sleep patterns. For example, dreams are often suppressed by lack of sleep or the use of drugs to induce sleep. Another possibility recommended by Morton Kelsey is to try praying for a dream. Interestingly, Tristine Rainer cites a number of secular parallels: she suggests that it is possible to invoke dreams from what she calls your 'sleeping self'.

Would it not be better to keep a separate dream journal? Quite a number of people do this and it certainly makes it easy to review your dreams and look for patterns within them. Carl Jung was a great advocate of this practice and it has been further refined by Ira Progoff. However, if you accept the principle that dreams are primarily concerned with aspects of your own life this approach has the disadvantage that it takes them out of context. On the whole, I believe that it is better to integrate your recollection of dreams into your journal record of your daily life. This need not be an obstacle to reviewing your dreams since there are a number of techniques you can use to make them stand out within your journal. Tristine Rainer suggests that you give each dream a short descriptive title and keep a separate index of dream titles. Alternatively, you could write down your dreams in a different colour (I use green) or use a highlighter to make them stand out.

Reviewing your dreams

Since we are talking about spiritual journalling, this should be done in a context of prayer. One of the principles which the Bible lays down for its approach to dreams is that the interpretation of a dream belongs to God (Gen. 40:8). Any spiritual insight which might arise from a dream is to be regarded as a gift of God.

The simplest way to review a particular dream is probably to apply something like the Ignatian method to your notes. In other words, relive the dream in God's presence, elaborating it where necessary with the help of your imagination and keeping brief notes of the process in your journal. It may be helpful to keep certain questions in mind as you do so. For example, is there a clear message in the dream: do you recall any words which were spoken within the dream? What is your general impression of the dream? Who are the characters in your dream? Are they people you know or are they in some sense symbolic? (Jung mentions a number of symbolic characters who appeared and reappeared in his dreams as the conveyors of wisdom and insight). Are there any impersonal symbols (like Kekulé's snakes) in your dream?

How are we to interpret such symbols? It is possible to gain some insight from dictionaries of mythological and dream symbols. However, since the meaning of such symbols is to a large extent determined by the circumstances and psyche of the dreamer, these can only be of very limited help. To my mind, there are two ways forward. It is possible to gain some insight into the specific meaning of a symbol by entering into an imaginative dialogue with it. Clearly this is easier when the symbol is a living being. However, it should still be borne in mind that, for the Christian, the interpretation ultimately belongs to God. This suggests that the most direct way is to pray for insight and meditate upon the contents of the dream.

'This is all very well but I have a job and family. I just don't have the time to do all this meditation.' I can well believe that many people might react like this because it was precisely my reaction when I started to pursue my interest in journal keeping and dreams. Jung's account of his encounter with dreams was particularly daunting. Apparently he spent a significant amount of time every day for several years analysing his own dreams. That may be appropriate if you are in training to become a Jungian analyst but it is out of the question for most of us. All I am suggesting is that you may find it helpful to use your journal to replay any dreams you feel are particularly significant or which tantalise or worry you.

In the case of disturbing dreams and nightmares, reliving them in a prayerful context can be a very helpful way of tackling them. As you re-enter the nightmare, you can do so conscious that you are not alone. Imagine that Jesus is present within the nightmare with you, protecting you and helping you bring the whole thing to a positive resolution.

In addition to the immediate benefits of being able to tackle frightening dreams in this way, prayerful review of your dreams offers a number of longer term benefits. You may find that a particular dream is helpful in enabling you to make some decision.

Or you may find that it brings you fresh insights of one sort or another. But, above all, examining your dreams in the presence of God is one more avenue for increasing self-knowledge and personal growth.

I should, however, add that while for the average normal person this is a perfectly harmless and insightful procedure there are situations in which it may be wise not to undertake such analysis on your own. Again, taking the example of Jung, it is apparent from his *Memories, Dreams, Reflections* that the psychic forces he unleashed were so great as to prove a real threat to his own sanity. He weathered the storm but such experiences amongst the pioneers of psychoanalysis convinced them that self-analysis should not be done in isolation. If you fear or even suspect that such dream analysis might throw up more than you are prepared to handle, I would recommend that you leave well alone (or, better, find someone you can trust to support you, e.g., your vicar, elder, or spiritual director). This is true of other aspects of journal keeping as well: if you feel reluctant to pursue a particular line, respect that reluctance. It may well be that you are not yet ready to turn over that particular stone.

PRAYERFUL DAYDREAMING

If you are suspicious of journal keeping, you may well feel that your suspicions have just been confirmed; that journal keeping is a form of escapism. Daydreaming and fantasy are dirty words in many Christian circles. At best such habits are regarded as a self-indulgent escape from reality which leaves you unfit for taking part in the spiritual warfare of the Church. At worst they are suspected of leaving you open to the influence of psychic or occult forces.

The arguments which are used against daydreaming are similar to those employed against the reading of fantasy literature and the playing of games like 'Dungeons and Dragons'.

One argument is that daydreams are escapist. C. S. Lewis dismisses the charge of escapism against fantasy literature in the following terms:

> I never fully understood it till my friend Professor Tolkien asked me the very simple question, 'What class of men would you expect to be most preoccupied with, and most hostile to, the idea of escape?' and gave the obvious answer: jailers . . . [T]hose who brood much on the remote past or future, or stare long at the night sky, are less likely than others to be ardent or orthodox partisans.[2]

Daydreaming may be escapist but such escapism may be turned to our advantage, freeing us from imprisonment within our immediate concerns.

Others say daydreams leave us open to psychic and occult forces. Critics of fantasy are quick to point out horror stories such as the Manson family's pseudo-religion based on the novel *Stranger in a Strange Land*. The cruder forms of such criticism simply assume that any reference to magic is dangerous. Thus Christian leaders stand up and condemn *The Lord of the Rings*! This is particularly ironic since, although it never mentions God, it is a profoundly religious book and, indeed, reading that book as a student was one of the factors which led to my own conversion. More generally the idea that a particular class of literature, or game, or the mere exercise of imagination in daydreaming can, of itself, open us to evil is fundamentally misguided. I do not

2. *Of This and Other Worlds*, Fount 1984, p. 89.

doubt that perverted fantasy novels and games exist. Nor do I doubt that daydreams can be perverted. But the fact that perversions exist should not be used as a blanket condemnation. If that were not so, Christianity could be condemned on account of perversions within the Church!

Daydreaming and fantasy are suspected by many Christians but nowhere more than when they appear in prayer. There is a long tradition of warning against daydreaming in prayer. It is something to be resisted and, if you find yourself unable to resist, it is something to be confessed. Writers on prayer and spirituality offer us a variety of techniques for suppressing such daydreams. These range from simple prayers for victory (which are supposed to provide us with automatic protection from the Satanic influence of daydreams) to elaborate rituals of recollection intended to aid our withdrawal from all worldly concerns. But, if we suppress our imaginations in this way perhaps we shall create significant gaps in our prayers. Sometimes the very things which we most need to bring before God are most clearly expressed in our daydreams and fantasies. If we refuse to acknowledge them before God, we may be denying those aspects of our lives which we find shameful or embarrassing or frightening.

The value of daydreams

Imagination and its expression in dreams, daydreams and fantasies are, I believe, an important part of what it is to be human. Imagination is an essential part of both human freedom and creativity. Thus it is bound up with our likeness to God.

Daydreaming can be of real positive value because of the place it occupies between conscious thought and dreaming. We can actively manipulate our day-dreams (something which most of us cannot do with nocturnal dreams). But daydreams are like dreams in that they can reveal to us much that lies beyond the usual horizon of consciousness. If we examine the content of our daydreams we may well discover much about things that concern us deeply: our sexuality, our anxieties, our resentments, our preferred forms of self-gratification. Often our daydreams reflect the things that really matter to us: if your prayers are regularly interrupted by daydreams about what X has done perhaps you should take a hint and start praying for X (or perhaps you should stop praying and seek out X in order to settle the matter: Matt. 5:23f). It may be that our daydreams will give rise to a strong awareness of our own sinfulness. But surely that is no reason to dismiss them from our prayers. On the contrary, if that is the case, we should be all the more concerned to lay our daydreams before God.

Daydreams and journal keeping

Because of the similarity between dreams and daydreams all that I have said about the one can also be applied to the other. It is quite legitimate to use your journal to keep tabs on what you, in fact, daydream about. These notes then allow you to work with your daydreams much as you would with nocturnal dreams.

However, it is possible to take a more active approach to daydreaming in your journal. One way is to extend the Ignatian method of Bible meditation to tackle any issue which concerns you. This is the approach adopted by the Jesuit writer Anthony de

Mello. It is similar in many respects to the journalling technique known as guided imagery.

Tristine Rainer recommends that someone coming to guided imagery for the first time might begin with a meditation upon an ideal location: any physical space which for you represents peace and tranquillity. It may be a sunny beach, or a mountain meadow, or the stillness of a Gothic cathedral. Quieten yourself and build up a mental image of that place. Now withdraw in your imagination into that place. Spend a few minutes there experiencing it with all your imaginative senses; absorbing the peace of that place. Note as many details of the place as possible. Look at what you are feeling.

Now return to the present. You may find the contrast with your daydream painful. However, Anthony de Mello suggests that if you repeat the exercise several times you will begin to find the peace and tranquillity of the daydream spilling over into real life.

Once you have created such a place you can begin to elaborate your daydream in various ways. Rainer suggests that you populate it with imaginary people and animals. From a Christian perspective a more satisfactory way of developing it would be to turn it into a place of prayer: a place where in your imagination you can meet with Jesus.

That is one very simple form of prayerful daydreaming and I shall give you one or two more ideas in the exercises at the end of the chapter but the possibilities are endless.

Another approach which is widely used in contemporary journal keeping is the dialogue. One of the commonest forms of daydreaming is the replaying of conversations you have had. Very often this begins 'If only I had said . . .' and proceeds to imagine a devastating put down or a situation in which you did not miss that opportunity or in which you did ask her out.

The earliest example I know of dialogue as a journal technique is to be found in the journal of the nineteenth-century French novelist George Sand. She used to converse with an imaginary Dr Piffoel. However, current use of the technique derives mainly from the Gestalt school of psychotherapy and the work of Ira Progoff. Strictly speaking it is a form of active daydreaming but because of its importance as a tool for actively developing your relationship with others I shall leave discussion of it until chapter 6, 'The Outward-looking Journal'.

By way of conclusion let me just repeat that imagination, dreams and daydreams are not to be feared and suppressed. Just because imagination is such a powerful aspect of the human psyche, such suppression is the very thing which could turn it into something fearful. If you deny it, you may find that your imagination breaks out of the prison you have created at the most inopportune times. If you affirm it, you will be able to train it in directions which lead to personal growth and self-fulfilment. Your journal can be an invaluable tool in that process of affirmation and training.

Exercises

(i) Baptism

Begin by using one of the preparation exercises suggested in chapter 3; become still inside and out; admit to God your dependence upon him, and ask for his guidance as you explore the experience of baptism.

Read Mark 1:1–11 a couple of times, slowly and reflectively. Does any word or phrase seem particularly striking to you? If so, note it down and bear it in mind as you go on to the next stage of the exercise.

Build up a mental picture of the scene depicted in the passage. Imagine that you are part of the crowd meeting by the Jordan to be baptised by John. Jot down a brief description of the scene: what can you see? hear? feel? taste? smell? Take plenty of time to imagine what each one of your senses might be telling you about the scene.

It is your turn to be baptised. You stand in the water before John. What is the water like? Is it clear or murky? warm or cold? inviting or repelling? What are your feelings about the prospect of baptism?

Now imagine him thrusting you into that water. Feel it closing over your head.

Then it is all over. What are your feelings after the event?

On the basis of this imagined experience, reflect on the significance of baptism in your life. What does your baptism mean for you now? *From* what has it set you free? *For* what has it set you free? (Your response to these questions could take the form of short paragraphs or itemised lists.)

Where has your baptism put you in relation to God, the Church, your family, the world? (If you like, this question could be answered by drawing a diagram or sketch.)

Finally, review what you have written. Does anything in particular strike you (either in what you have noted down or in what you have omitted)?

(ii) The road to Calvary

As before, begin by relaxing and becoming aware of God's presence. When you are ready, ask the Holy Spirit to guide your reflections on this passage.

Read Mark 10:32–45 twice, slowly and reflectively. Note down any words or phrases which seem particularly striking.

Build up a mental image of the road to Jerusalem. Is it early or late in the day? Is it hot? Is the road dusty? or stony? or sandy?

Imagine that you are part of Jesus' entourage as he makes what is likely to be his last journey to Jerusalem. Where are you in relation to him? Look for him. Is he near at hand? Or has he been hanging back talking to one or two of the disciples? Or perhaps, he has walked on ahead of you. What are your feelings about such a journey? Note down those feelings.

Spend a few minutes thinking about what you would like to get out of your faith, out of the Church, out of your vocation. Prepare a list of such items.

Now go to him and like James and John, petition him for one of the things on your list. What are your feelings as you approach him? How does he respond to your request? Allow his response to become the basis for an imaginative dialogue as you explore further the implications of your request. If time permits, you might like to introduce more items from your list.

(iii) Climbing the mountain of the Lord

As before, begin by relaxing and becoming aware of God's presence.

When you feel that you are ready, try to imagine

yourself climbing a steep hill or mountain. Feel the steepness of the slope and the strain it imposes on your leg muscles. Are you trying to carry anything up the hill? Look at the ground ahead of you. Is it a well worn path, or a grassy slope, or bare rock? Look upwards, ahead of you, at the summit towering above you. Look around and see, in your mind's eye, other mountains towering around. Do they seem to be closing in on you? Or do you have a sense of openness?

Imagine yourself climbing this slope for a few minutes. Now the slope begins to ease off. You are entering a narrow pass. Follow the pass and let your imagination reveal what is at the end of the pass. Describe who or what you find. If you meet a person, you could enter into an imaginative dialogue.

A variation on this exercise might be to focus on the pack you are carrying. Since this is the mountain of the Lord, this would be an opportunity to let your imagination describe any burdens or hindrances you are taking with you on the Christian journey. Another variation might be to think about your companions on that journey.

(iv) Terminal illness

Meditation on your own death is to be found in a number of spiritual traditions. Amongst other things it is a powerful tool for putting the various aspects of our life into perspective (and helping us not to be overwhelmed by the trivia of modern life).

Imagine yourself in the doctor's waiting room. You have come for the results of some tests. Build up a picture of the waiting room and of your feelings as you wait to know the outcome.

71

Picture yourself entering his (or her) office. You sit down. The doctor is full of compassion as he tells you that you are terminally ill. You have one month to live.

What is your reaction? Focus on your feelings for a while.

You leave the doctor's surgery and begin to walk down the street. Look at your surroundings. Describe them.

Where are you going? Do you want to talk to anyone? Who?

It is possible to extend this exercise almost indefinitely to examine the implications of your own mortality for every aspect of your life and for all your relationships.

5

Mapping Your Life

A common feature of nearly all personal journals is their role in helping their keepers make sense of their lives. Individual journal entries do this to some extent. Henri Nouwen writes of 'a day that is so fragmented that it does not seem to come together at all – except perhaps by writing about it!'[1] Furthermore, the entries in your journal can become the raw material for the process of creating a map of your life.

However, the journal entries are not themselves the map (or the autobiography). The poet Edwin Muir drew attention to the distinction in the first version of his *Autobiography* which he called *The Story and the Fable*. For Muir, the story is merely the retelling of what happened: the chronicle, the journal entries, the raw material. What really interests him is the fable: the interpretation which gives shape to the mass of details contained in the journal.

This is similar to what I mean by active autobiography. For me, autobiography is not merely the retelling of what happened but its interpretation. It means looking for the connections which make the entries in my journal hang together. Since leaving school I have studied astronomy, physics, and, more

1. *The Road to Daybreak: A Spiritual Journey*, p. 80.

recently, theology. I have been a schoolteacher, a university tutor, a father and househusband, a member of a Christian community, and a writer! Looked at from the outside, my life shows little evidence of shape or meaning. The autobiographical process which takes place in my journal plays an important role in bringing to light the hidden unity and significance of all those apparent changes of role and direction.

As a Christian, the discernment of God's providential care within those changes is an important unifying factor for me. In fact, I would be inclined to say that for Christians in general, the creation of an autobiography is really the preparation of a personal providential history.

However, people examine their pasts for many reasons, not all of them good. Few people ever attain a position of sufficient importance in society for a genuine historical interest to be their motive. Much more likely is a sentimental attachment to the past which results in people retelling over and over again their experiences of ten or twenty years ago. Still worse than sentimentality is fear of the future. Dwelling on the past can be a way of escaping from the demands of the present and the future.

For the Christian, the main motivation for examining their past should not be either of these. Nor is it simply an academic interest in the nature of God's providential activity. The primary reason for re-examining what God has been doing is so as to worship him better. Part and parcel of discerning God's providence is realising the extent to which you have cooperated with or resisted his will. It is a fact that the past helps to shape the present: past thoughts and deeds play a part in determining how you will think and act today, for good or ill. The recognition that you have formerly behaved in certain ways may help you to avoid falling back into the same old responses. Alternatively a prayerful re-examination of the past can sometimes give you pointers to the way ahead.

The chapters of your life

This process of seeking the meaning (providential or otherwise) in your personal history need not be confined to the period covered by your journal. On the contrary, your journal is an ideal place in which to begin the exploration of the further reaches of your past.

Probably no one has done more to develop this use of the personal journal than Ira Progoff. The discernment and investigation of the major phases of one's life form an essential part of his journal workshops.

His starting point is the listing of what he calls the 'Steppingstones' of a person's life. These are important moments in the movement of that life. They may be objective external events or inner experiences. They may arouse joyful memories and associations or recall traumatic events, moments of great pain. The title of Dag Hammarskjöld's journal, *Markings*, suggests the same thing. As a keen mountaineer, it was natural for him to choose a metaphor from climbing: whenever you attempt a previously uncharted climb you leave markers behind you to record where you have been. Steppingstones or markings are the landmarks which enable you to retrace the path you have taken up to the present day. They are the chapter headings for the fable of your life.

The procedure for creating a list of markings or chapter headings is similar to that of the listing exercises in chapter 3. When you are relaxed, try to discern the movement of your life. Imagine your life history spread out before you as a sort of mural. What is your overall impression? Do not focus on any particular aspect at this stage, simply try to feel the overall flow. It may be continuous, like a river; or a kaleidoscope of disconnected events.

When you have done this you are ready to prepare your list of chapter headings. As before, in order to keep the list manageable it is a good idea to limit it to no more than a dozen items. The first time you do this exercise it is helpful to put down one or two basic objective markers, e.g., 'I was born', 'I entered secondary school'. When you have done that, simply complete the list with whatever comes to mind. As ever, the point of letting the statements come spontaneously is to evade the workings of your internal censor. As an aid to spontaneity the chapter headings should be short: brief phrases or even key words. By the same token, it is inadvisable to impose any kind of order on the list.

They need not mean anything to an outsider, and they need not be chronological. Whatever you produce will be a spontaneously selected list of titles for significant periods in your life history. Reading through the list gives an overview of your life from your vantage point in the present.

'But what if I overlook important events and experiences which are buried in my past?' I would reply that such anxieties are unfounded. The list you have prepared is not an exercise in objective scientific history. On the contrary, it is a list of those items which seem most important to you from your present vantage point. As your vantage point changes, your perceptions of what has been important in your life will also change. Thus this is an exercise which can fruitfully be repeated many times.

Exploring the past

Progoff uses the 'Steppingstones' list to create a framework around which you can build up a picture of your life history. It provides an outline sketch which can be filled in later by further reflection in your journal.

Having prepared your list, the next step is to explore each item in more detail. Each 'Steppingstone' may be regarded as pointing to a specific period or phase of your life. As a starting point, you could re-read your list and choose that one which seems most significant, most interesting, or most intriguing to you at this moment.

As you turn that chapter heading over in your mind, observe and note down whatever it evokes. What events come to mind? Do you connect any particular individuals with that period? Any images? Emotions? What was the feel of the period? If you have the time to do so, Progoff recommends that you continue your reflections until you have exhausted all your conscious memories of the period.

However, this process of 'time stretching' is just one way in which you can use a personal journal to explore your past. There is also considerable scope for the use of your imagination here. For example, you might consider writing imaginative journal entries for periods in your life which you now regard as particularly significant. This could be done with the help of the techniques described in the previous chapter (particularly the section on prayerful daydreaming). Instead of using a biblical text or other piece of writing, you could use striking memories, childhood photographs or other mementos as the basis for the imaginative recreation of scenes from your own past.

Another possibility is to enter into imaginative dialogues with your former self. These may arise spontaneously as you keep your journal. For example, you may find that, while heeding Tristine Rainer's advice to write fast and put down whatever comes, you begin to write things which your conscious mind would not endorse. Do these journal 'voices' represent a childish (or childlike) point of view? If so, it may be that you have uncovered aspects of yourself which have been suppressed. Dialogue with these 'voices' may be useful in deepening your understanding of your personal history. Alternatively, you may adopt a more deliberate approach based on the imaginative recreation described above. As you build up the scene in your mind, imagine that you are an observer rather than the child at the centre of the events. As a sympathetic adult you could enter into an imaginative dialogue with the child you once were.

Healing the past

The above reference to journal 'voices' leads naturally to this topic. As you continue such explorations you may stumble across dark memories: moments of pain, confusion, or shame which are still festering away in the recesses of your personality. Active exploration of these dark corners through a journal can be a powerful way of exposing them to the light and enabling you to find healing. The therapeutic value of journals is amply demonstrated by the existence of bereavement journals such as C. S. Lewis's *A Grief Observed*. Journalling may also be a way of coping with other forms of bereavement, e.g., redundancy.

There is no reason why the above techniques for reconstructing your personal history should not be used to tackle painful events and suppressed memories. However, as a Christian, this is not something I would attempt alone. Healing and salvation are intimately linked by the New Testament. Thus, such therapeutic journal keeping would be most appropriate in the context of prayer. For example, the imaginative reconstruction outlined above could be treated as an Ignatian style meditation on a particular memory, experience, or guilt. Remembering the universality of Christ's healing presence, you could invite him to accompany you as an active participant in your journey of exploration.

I am conscious that there may be dangers involved in such explorations. This is particularly true of attempts to carry on dialogues with personalised psychic forces. In his autobiography, the analyst Carl Jung describes his own journey into the unconscious thus:

> I stood helpless before an alien world; everything in it seemed difficult and incomprehensible. I was living in a constant state of tension; often I felt as if gigantic blocks of stone were tumbling down upon me. One thunderstorm followed another. Others have been shattered by them – Nietzsche, and Hölderlin, and many others.[2]

Elsewhere he says that only the support of his family and his professional commitments enabled him to retain his sanity.

Clearly it would be dangerous to stray into such

2. *Memories, Dreams and Reflections*, p. 201.

areas. However, there need be no danger in journal keeping so long as you trust the promptings of your conscience and discernment at all times. If you feel at all uneasy about anything that your journal keeping exposes, you should leave well alone. Anything like that is better explored in close cooperation with someone you trust (e.g., your pastor, priest, elder, or spiritual director).

THE JOURNAL AS CONFESSOR

Closely related to the therapeutic role of the journal is its role as confessor.

Confession has been a divisive issue within the Christian churches. Thanks mainly to widespread mediaeval abuses, there is an abiding suspicion of the practice amongst Protestants. It is regarded as superstitious, verging on the magical with its suggestion that God may be manipulated into forgiving you by appropriate acts of contrition. It is accused of failing to take sin seriously enough, allowing people to exorcise their guilt without any radical change of life-style. It may also be dismissed as a morbid practice encouraging excessive self-criticism.

And yet, confession in one form or another has been virtually universal amongst those who sought to take the Christian life seriously. Where the Roman Catholic practice of sacramental confession has been frowned on, confession itself has still flourished. Perhaps nowhere was this more true than amongst the Puritans on both sides of the Atlantic. Public confession and the penitents' bench were a regular feature of worship. They confessed their sins to one another. Above all they confided their sins to their journals.

But what is confession? The greatest misunderstanding of confession is to treat it on its own. It is never something that a Christian indulges in for its own sake. It is certainly not a psychological form of self-flagellation. On the contrary, it is an integral part of the process of repentance. It is the conscious recognition and admission that the path you are taking is not one which God would have you take. Such recognition is the daily starting point for anyone who is seriously intent on following God.

Thus confession is the very opposite of a morbid concern for the past. Such an attitude would be a clear symptom that something was wrong. No, confession is the verbal expression of the very positive activity of preparing for the future by means of realistic self-examination.

The role of the journal

Clearly a journal is one secure means of expressing the results of your self-examination. Such expression is valuable because it helps to make your self-examination concrete and specific. There is a world of difference between mere repetition of the general confession or the litany and the sort of highly personal and quite specific confession which you can make in the pages of a journal (or to another human being). Only the latter creates the possibility for specific repentance and the taking of appropriate action.

Examples of specific personal confession abound in spiritual journals: David Brainerd, John Wesley, Henry Martyn, Jim Elliott, Henri Nouwen to name but a few.

The great advantage of using your journal as a confessor is that re-reading enables you to see areas in which your life has really changed. It also reveals starkly and objectively those habits and attitudes of which you feel guilty but which you are unwilling to give up. By providing you with a record of progress and failure the journal adds depth to the activity of self-examination: it allows you to put your current concerns, anxieties and sense of guilt into perspective.

Thus it makes it easier for you to engage in a systematic programme of self-examination in which you gradually scrutinise every aspect of your personality, behaviour and relationships.

The method described earlier for creating the chapter headings of your personal history can easily be adapted as a starting point for such a process of self-examination. As always it is advisable to begin by relaxing and seeking God's presence and guidance before beginning. Instead of focussing on the overall flow of your life you should concentrate on the things which are currently disturbing your life. This could be repeated for different aspects of your life resulting in several lists. For example, you might want to list your greatest fears, your strongest desires, your most disturbing doubts, the things of which you are most ashamed, or the things which fill you with pride. Remember, the point of the exercise is self-examination not self-criticism.

Armed with these lists you are ready to tackle specific doubts, fears, etc. It is highly unlikely that any of the items you have listed will have appeared suddenly and inexplicably in your life within the past few years! In other words, every one of these items will have a history. It is possible to apply Progoff's 'Steppingstones' technique to each of these histories in just the same way as it is applied to the overall flow of your life. Having chosen the item you wish to explore further, focus on the impact it has had on your personal history and prepare chapter headings for its history within your life story. The techniques described in the section on 'Active Autobiography' may then be deployed to explore those periods, to reconstruct your experience of that particular fear, or doubt, or sin, and where necessary to seek Christ's healing for your past.

Of course this is by no means the only approach which you might adopt. One alternative would be to use your journal for working through a list of personal questions designed to make you reflect on your response to God's action in your life. Perhaps the best known is the Examen in Ignatius of Loyola's *Spiritual Exercises*. Similar lists will be found in several of the books mentioned in the Appendix.

TAKING RESPONSIBILITY

I originally intended to call this section 'Regaining Control of Your Life'. Had this been a book about secular journal keeping techniques that title would have sufficed. However, the journal as an expression of the Christian life cannot be satisfied with merely regaining control for oneself.

In the back of my mind as I write are the peculiar pressures which modern society imposes upon us. One of the most deplorable features of our enterprise culture is the tendency to believe that unless you are a financial success, you are a personal failure. And the fundamental condition of success is total devotion to work. In order to be successful today, men and women will work in the evenings and at the weekends at the expense of their personal relationships.

Nor are Christians immune from this pressure. They may well find that their employers demand that they put work before their marriages or their church commitments. A former acquaintance of mine who worked for a multinational corporation was given a month's notice to move to the Far East. Of course his employers made sure he would not lose out financially but what about the friendships that were broken off as a result, and what about the church which lost a valuable youth worker?

Alongside this pressure to worship success, there is the pressure created by our society's loss of values. Those who still attempt to commend particular values lack the authority to do so. To those who disagree with them their values appear to be arbitrary and to demand submission to their will. A generation ago Christians complained that our society recognised only scientific truths. Today even those are doubted and perhaps only economic 'truths' remain unquestioned. Again many voices of protest tell us that as a society we have lost all sense of beauty. Goodness, truth and beauty, the essential standards by which we see meaning in life, have evaporated. Little wonder that for so many our enterprise culture should seem ultimately meaningless.

The journal and problem solving

Even before I began keeping a journal seriously I would use scraps of paper to help me in problem solving. Lists of advantages and disadvantages can be helpful in making a decision. Writing can be an invaluable aid in analysing scientific or business problems. But journal keeping can extend the problem solving capacity of writing into the personal realm.

One way in which journal keeping can help you is by enabling you to express your feelings about the problem. Indeed the very act of admitting the problem to yourself and God in the pages of the journal can itself be a healing experience.

Having admitted the problem it is possible to use the security of the journal to express your frustration, anger, guilt, fear, or whatever other emotions the situation engenders. There is no need to put a brave or respectable face on your feelings when you are confiding to yourself and God in this way.

The most immediate way to tackle the problem is simply to describe your feelings about it. However, it is possible to adopt a more imaginative approach if you feel so inclined. That old standby of journal keepers, the unsent letter, is an ideal vehicle for this sort of expressive writing. In the privacy of your journal, you can write to your employer, your vicar, your lover, or your parents expressing what you really feel about them.

Alternatively, you could attempt to come to terms with the problem through less realistic forms of fantasy. For example, you could personalise the problem and enter into an imaginative dialogue with it; or you could try writing a fairy story (or some other appropriate piece of fiction) which embodies it. Yet another possibility is to use the pages of your journal in order to draw what you feel about it.

Such expressive writing will help you feel better about the problem. It may help you to put it in perspective. It may even help you to live with it. In these ways it can be an invaluable aid in overcoming the paralysis which so often afflicts people faced with major problems. But, for all its usefulness, expressive writing can only be a preliminary stage in dealing with your problems (personal or otherwise). If not, one may begin to suspect that the journal is being used to escape reality rather than to face it.

Problem solving as opposed to merely learning to live with the situation demands that you attempt to analyse the problem. This simply means that you must attempt to break it down into manageable portions. This is as true for personal problems as it is for problems in school physics. And a major cause of failure in both types of problem solving is lack of such analysis.

Perhaps a particular problem may be analysed in several different ways. That doesn't matter. All you need is for the problem to be analysed in one way. The important thing is a solution. Don't waste time trying to find the most elegant solution.

Yet again the 'Steppingstones' technique may be helpful. You could try outlining the history of the problem in this way. By exploring the various phases of its development you are likely to find specific things you could do to tackle parts of the problem. Thus the journal can be an aid in clarifying problems and helping you to find ways of tackling aspects of those problems. Of course, you must still take the action suggested by your journal keeping.

Giving control to Christ

According to research based on the theory of psychological types, people are about equally divided into those who want to control their world and those who want to experience it. For the former, allowing life to control you is a clear indication of personal (and spiritual) failure. It is hardly surprising, therefore, that most, if not all, books on successful management are really about techniques to enable the readers to regain control of their lives.

However, the Christian life is based on different criteria of success. Instead of being able to control one's own destiny in order to achieve personal and financial success, the Christian standard of success is the fruit of the Spirit. And this is a standard which neither submission to external authorities (such as the church, the state or the company) nor control over one's destiny can ever achieve.

Submission is involved, but it is purely internal. God promised to write a new law on our hearts. Christian submission is directed not to human authorities nor even to an external God. Rather it is directed to the God who, through the Holy Spirit, dwells within every Christian.

Once again, the imaginative use of the journal offers an aid to handing over control of one's life to Christ. This may take the form of appropriate meditations in which we imagine ourselves offering Christ our successes, our decisions, etc. Alternatively, if you are one of those for whom experience takes priority over control, you may prefer to use such meditations to help your experiences to be more God centred.

DECISIONS, DISCERNMENT AND GUIDANCE

Prayerful planning

This subtitle embodies the paradox of the Christian life. It is precisely parallel to Paul's advice to 'work out your salvation with fear and trembling, for it is

God who works in you to will and to act according to his good purpose' (Phil. 2:12–13 NIV). On the one hand, we are called to take responsibility for our own lives. God does not expect us to give up that responsibility to others. Indeed such handing over of control to other Christians could well be interpreted as burying a very important talent God has given every one of us. God calls us to plan our own spiritual pilgrimages. On the other hand, we must do so recognising that our very ability to plan is part of God's gift of humanity and that God remains in ultimate control.

With that paradox in mind, we turn to a number of journal keeping techniques which may be of help in making decisions about the future.

Mapping the future

As always, such decision making must be prayerful if it is to be regarded as a spiritual exercise. Christians sometimes speak of seeking God's will (or divine guidance) as if it were something strange and mysterious. Such ways of speaking create a great deal of unnecessary misunderstanding for those who have recently embarked on the Christian life. In reality the only difference between secular decision making and seeking God's will is that the latter is decision making steeped in prayer.

Some readers might object that seeking divine guidance must involve listening for the voice of God to speak either internally, or through Scripture, or some other means. I would not deny that, but I regard it as an integral part of prayer and not something which is exclusive to prayers for guidance. To make decisions in a prayerful context is to remember that God is the senior partner in every decision.

He is intimately involved in every detail of your planning.

I have already mentioned in passing one simple decision making device, namely, pro and con lists. After you have gathered whatever information you feel is necessary for a decision, simply sit down and, conscious of God's presence and guidance, list all the advantages and disadvantages you can perceive in each of the possible courses of action. You may well find that it is necessary to give some sort of subjective weighting to each of the items (perhaps highlighting the major advantages and disadvantages). Of course such a device can become very complex if you are faced with a major personal decision (e.g., getting married, changing jobs, moving house). Nevertheless, with that proviso I have found such lists to be very helpful in my decision making.

Sometimes new insights into the future may be found by re-examining past decisions. Once again this is an approach which Ira Progoff has developed with an exercise called 'Roads taken/not taken'. The point of such exercises is not a sentimental reliving of the past but to learn lessons for the present from past decisions. Progoff uses the exercise to uncover unlived possibilities: all those things we might have done and been had we chosen differently. Such 'might-have-beens' contain implications for how we live now and what we might do in the future. He encourages journal keepers to use their journals to explore the process of decision making in a manner similar to that already described. In such explorations we may ask ourselves, what did I choose not to do when I chose to do X? For example, my decision to become a teacher involved a decision to give up research. The decision to pursue a particular pastime might involve forgoing another. It is worth re-examining those unlived possibilities occasionally to see whether circumstances have changed and what was then inappropriate has become appropriate.

Finally, it is possible to adopt a more imaginative approach to thoughts about the future. This may be particularly helpful for very complex decisions which defy the sort of analysis already described. Once again the techniques of prayerful daydreaming are appropriate. Taking each of the possible alternatives (and perhaps some impossible ones too) as the basis for your meditations you can use your journal as a way of exploring your feelings about each of these possible futures. One way is by entering into dialogues with each of your future selves. Another way is by 'remembering' the future: imaginatively building up a picture of a typical day in the future (perhaps ten years from now) and writing a journal entry for that day. Such methods may help you to establish which of the possibilities you feel most comfortable with.

Exercises

(i) My earliest memory

As usual, begin by relaxing using one of the methods suggested in earlier chapters.

When you are ready, cast your mind back to your childhood. What is your earliest memory? Don't worry if it is only an isolated fragment, one of the purposes of this exercise is to demonstrate the capacity of the imagination to expand such fragments.

Use that memory to locate yourself in that period

of childhood. Use your imagination to recall what your surroundings were like. What did they look like to your child's eyes? Recall and record the sensations you experienced in as much detail as possible. Try to build up a picture of the house you lived in. Where did you sleep? Did you have a cot or a bed? Did you share the room? If so, with whom? Where did you eat? Where did that first memory occur? How big were you? Try to recall impressions of size from that period of childhood: your own hand in an adult's, the size of an adult's chair.

When you are satisfied with your imaginative description of that period of early childhood take some time to reflect on its contents. It is sometimes said that your earliest memory is a key to understanding your entire life. Does that seem to be true in your case?

(ii) Death and transfiguration

The aim of this exercise is to investigate some of the personal changes we are continually experiencing.

As usual, begin by relaxing. Let yourself become aware of God's presence. He is with you in the midst of all the changes and uncertainties of life. Ask the Holy Spirit for insight as you engage in the exercise.

Begin by making a list of at least five items that you feel are dying in your life, the things you feel diminishing, becoming less important, receding, separating, the things you are losing interest in, letting go of, things that seem just about over. Perhaps you once enjoyed gardening but are beginning to find it drudgery. Perhaps a friendship or a job seems to be coming to an end. Perhaps an old attitude or feeling is changing. Concentrate on things that seem to be passing but are not completely past.

Begin a second list of things that are coming into being, things that are not fully a part of your life but which are rising, emerging, returning, becoming more important, more desirable. This might include a new friendship, or job.

Take a couple of minutes to look over your completed lists. Select from each list the one item which seems most significant or interesting to you. Take half an hour or so to write about these items. Tell the story of that which is waxing or waning, your feelings about it, anxieties, anticipations, expectations. Try to let your perceptions and feelings flow freely until they come to a natural conclusion. What is helping or hindering the passing of the old and the emergence of the new? What does this suggest to you?

If you have time, you might like to repeat the process for other items on the list. Do you see any connections between the two lists? If so, you might like to write about this relationship.

Review what you have written. Make any further notes or comments which suggest themselves. Ask God to show you his active presence in these changes. Does he appear to be pruning away some of these parts of your life in order to make room for fresh growth?

6

The Outward-looking Journal

I hope it is clear from previous chapters that journal keeping is not a panacea. Contrary to the impression created by some of its advocates, it is not necessarily a high road to personal and spiritual growth. Nor will it transform you overnight into a creative genius. It is no more than a tool, albeit a tool which I find particularly helpful. In the end growth depends not on the tool but on the willingness of its user to grow and to allow God to transform graciously him or her.

Besides that general point, journal keeping has a number of specific limitations and potential dangers. I have already mentioned these in passing. Now I want to summarise them and explore a vital corrective for the most important ones, namely, introspection and escapism.

Honesty

As I have said before, this is a fundamental condition of any serious personal or spiritual exploration through journal keeping. It is equally vital to every other approach to spirituality. The extent to which you are prepared to be honest with yourself and with God marks out the boundaries of your current potential for personal and spiritual growth. Clearly

93

you cannot grow in those areas you are not prepared to recognise or discuss.

I think there are two opposite dangers related to honesty. One is active dishonesty in journal keeping the self-delusion which causes you to idealise your self in the pages of your journal. The danger is that you can find yourself believing the false picture you have painted of yourself in the pages of your journal

Another form of self-delusion might be called the 'Chief of Sinners' syndrome. This is the use of the journal to castigate yourself for all sorts of imagined sins and personal shortcomings.

The opposite danger is failure to respect those internal boundaries. There are some who in pursuit of an ideal of complete honesty do great damage to themselves. This is the ever present danger of any form of self-analysis. The desire to leave no stone unturned can become an obsession which exposes the sufferer to hidden psychological and spiritual problems which he or she cannot handle alone.

Escapism

Closely related to the danger of self-delusion is the use of the journal as a way of escaping from reality The journal keeper's relationship with his or her journal can become a substitute for the more demanding task of developing relationships with other human beings and with God. A possible example of this danger would be the life of the Danish philosopher Kierkegaard. Over the years he invested a great deal of time and energy in his journal and other writing. However, it clearly did not help him develop real personal relationships. On the contrary there seems to be a close connection between his obsessive writing and his broken engagement.

That such introspective escapism is not the inevitable result of keeping a personal journal is clear from *The Diary* of Anne Frank. For her, Kitty (the name she gave her diary) became a paper confidante which enabled her to maintain and develop her relationships with her companions in hiding.

Journal keeping can also become a substitute for action. This certainly seems to be true of some journals written in the confessional style. One gets the impression that for their keepers the act of writing about their misdemeanours was a sufficient act of 'repentance'. Contrast the way in which Dr Johnson moans about the same petty faults year after year with the inner development of a David Brainerd or a Jim Elliott. The latter acted on the insights they gained from writing in their journals.

Addiction and possession

Morton Kelsey in his book on journal keeping warns that the practice can be addictive. This is certainly borne out by experienced journal keepers. Perhaps it is this characteristic which has allowed it to become a substitute for other more dangerous addictions. For example, the American organisation Eaters Anonymous encourages its members to tackle their compulsive eating through the medium of a journal.

Generally speaking, journal keepers find that the habit is a positive addiction on a par with regular exercise. However, for those who use it as an escape from the demands and responsibilities of reality it can take on some of the qualities of a negative addiction. Anaïs Nin used to describe her journal as her 'Kief, hashish, and opium'. Alone that phrase might be no more than a particularly colourful way of describing the journal keeper's dependence on journal keeping. However, elsewhere she admits to suffering from physical withdrawal symptoms when her analyst, Otto Rank, recommended a period of abstinence from journal keeping.

Personally, I believe that such obsessive journal keeping is relatively rare. Most journal keepers seem able to take it up or drop it as circumstances require. However, if you should find that you start to become anxious or irritable when you are prevented from making entries in your journal I would advise you to put your journal away and seek advice or support. Of course, this is equally true of any other spiritual discipline: if it seems to be becoming part of an obsessive behaviour pattern, it is time to stop and ask what is going wrong.

Related to the issue of addiction to journal keeping is what one might call the danger of possession. Again, I believe this is relatively unlikely. The joint safeguards of respecting the limits of your honesty and treating the whole exercise as a Christian spiritual discipline carried out for the glory of God and under the guidance and protection of the Holy Spirit should be sufficient protection. To ignore such safeguards is to risk possession by subconscious psychic (or demonic) forces. But this would be true whatever spiritual discipline individuals chose to pursue. It is not the tool but the user who must bear the responsibility. There are documented examples of such possession occurring in conjunction with charismatic worship. Today only a few extremists would lay the blame on the form of worship. It is what comes from within that corrupts.

Correctives

The dangers and limitations of journal keeping are precisely the same as any other form of self-analysis or solo spiritual discipline. Likewise the correctives are the same.

Contemporary psychoanalysts have discovered by trial and error that self-analysis without support is fraught with psychic dangers. They have simply rediscovered an aspect of a Christian truth which has largely been lost in our society. That truth is that human beings are largely constituted by their relationships (with one another, with their environment, and with God). They are not, contrary to the dominant secular philosophy of western society, ultimately isolated individuals. It follows that no practice which encourages such individualism can help us become more human.

Within the Christian churches the balance to all individual spiritual disciplines has always been the recognition that we are members one of another. We may pray, read our Bibles, meditate, and keep our journals in private. But what we do in private is never simply our own private affair. On the contrary, it always has public implications because it affects our relationships with one another. If I have been using my journal destructively to nourish a grudge against my vicar, that will have a public payoff in the form of broken relationships within the congregation. Conversely, if I use my journal to explore the reasons for that grudge, to seek forgiveness and ways of transforming that relationship the outcome will be the strengthening of relationships.

One way of encouraging the constructive use of the journal is to use it in conjunction with some form of spiritual support. The traditional form of this has been the individual spiritual director. This term may have a rather Roman Catholic ring to it but the practice is also to be found throughout the evangelical tradition. One of the greatest evangelical spiritual directors of the nineteenth century was Charles Simeon, who became a father in God to an entire generation of evangelical Anglican clergymen. More recently evangelical spiritual direction has been found under such titles as 'making disciples'.

Whatever you call it, the practice of developing a close relationship with a mature Christian is valuable for anyone who is serious about the Christian pilgrimage. Such a director, adviser, shepherd, or soul friend can warn you of potential pitfalls, and encourage you when the going is difficult. They are well-placed to prick the bubble of self-deception or to warn you when your spirituality is becoming too introspective or you are becoming obsessive about some practice.

The interdependence of Christians within the church means that it is not enough to seek support exclusively from an individual no matter how wise or holy that person may be. Ideally, the local congregation as a whole should be a network of mutual support. In practice this will mean that you relate with your fellow Christians at a variety of levels. You will find yourself leaning on some rather than others, and you will find that some are leaning on you. Today many churches encourage the development of such networks of practical mutual support through cell groups or housegroups.

Quite apart from the mutual support which is available through your local church, it is possible to take active measures to ensure that your journal is not simply an exercise in introspection. Various ways of encouraging such a consciously outward-looking

98

journal will be the main theme in the rest of this chapter.

The use of the journal to explore the highways and byways of your own psyche has become a major element in journal keeping in this century. However, as I pointed out in my introductory chapter, the present emphasis on introspective journal keeping is a relatively recent development. Journals have for centuries been used to describe, record, and capture for posterity various aspects of the external world. Chroniclers have faithfully recorded with little regard for their relative importance births, marriages, deaths, plagues and what they had for dinner! Explorers have supplemented their maps with careful accounts of their travels.

Anaïs Nin called her journals a way of saving memories. However the power of descriptive writing is such that a journal can be much more than a way of recording what has happened. The words you use to record events will later help to evoke your recollection of those events. Such personal descriptions of everyday experiences offer an important creative alternative to capturing them in photographs or on video. In fact, I have a friend who keeps a journal in preference to a photograph album. Ten years on, a brief paragraph detailing your reactions to Aunt Jessie's puce coat may be more illuminating than a fading snapshot of said relative wearing said article!

What you choose to record may be trivial in itself, like Aunt Jessie's coat. Or you may describe some of your formative experiences: your conversion, the birth of a child, the death of a close friend or relative. Whether the experience is trivial or of fundamental importance to you, a brief description will help you to relive it later. I have already said a good deal about reliving your past with a view to self-discovery. However, that is by no means the only reason for describing your world in your journal.

Another excellent reason for such descriptive writing is that such writing can become the basis for celebration and worship. Annie Dillard's *Pilgrim at Tinker Creek* is a marvellous example of this aspect of descriptive writing. Her observations of the changing seasons in the Blue Ridge Mountains become the basis for an extensive meditation on and celebration of God's creation.

The power of selectivity

Since what you write today will become the key to unlocking future memories of this day the simple daily record takes on a fresh importance. In a sense, what you write will become your history. This is strikingly underlined by the experience of the novelist Christopher Isherwood. As a young man in Weimar Germany he kept an intimate diary. This became the basis for a variety of novels, plays and films. However, he destroyed the diary itself. Years later when he came to write his autobiography he found that he could no longer trust his own memories of events because they had become interwoven with the fiction.

This recalls what I said before about using the journal to get at the myth or fable of your life. The contents of a journal are not the raw material for an objective chronology but for a personal interpretation. What you record and the way you record it will have an important influence on your later efforts at interpretation. By emphasising either the positive or the negative aspects of a chain of events it is possible to create two entirely different records.

No two journal keepers will record the same event in the same way. Imagine, for example, walking in the countryside in the pouring rain. One person will describe the sights and the smells and the sounds. Another will dwell on the misery of being cold and wet. Still another may worry about the risk of catching pneumonia.

Clearly the intention of a journal and its entries must be taken into account. People who keep journals mainly as places for letting off steam would be ill-advised to use such records as the basis for interpreting their life histories.

DIALOGUES WITH THE WORLD

I have already referred to the use of dialogues several times. This reflects its importance as a journal keeping device. And perhaps its most important application is in helping the development of relationships with the world around you.

Dialogues with people

These are, of course, the most natural type of dialogue. Potential journal keepers coming to the technique for the first time may be put off by the idea of imaginative dialogues with things, or events, or organisations, or parts of their body but most of them can see some potential in the idea of dialogues with people.

Within the pages of your journal it is possible to enter into dialogue with literally anyone. You can hold imaginary conversations with members of your family, friends, enemies, heroes, heroines, celebrities, politicians, characters out of history or fiction. The possibilities are limited only by the limits of your imagination.

If you have not tried it before, your reaction may be similar to my initial reaction. It sounds as if you are being asked to play chess against yourself. If you have ever tried that, you will know that it is relatively easy to play the opening moves honestly (they, after all, are well-documented in books about chess). However, as soon as you get into the middle game the temptation to favour one side becomes very strong (if not irresistible). I was surprised to find that the exercise was much more helpful than my suspicions led me to expect. The fundamental purpose of the technique is to help you enter imaginatively into someone else's thoughts and feelings, to put yourself in their position and try to feel their point of view as your own. My experience of journal dialogues is that they really do help you to understand the other person's point of view. However, it seems to be less effective when very strong feelings are involved. Then the temptation is to use the dialogue as a way of letting off steam rather than exploring alternative points of view. While that may be what is needed in the circumstances, it is unlikely to help you see the other person's point of view.

As I said, you can choose to hold imaginary conversations with anyone from your mother-in-law to the President of the United States or Gandalf the Grey. However, it will probably be most helpful to begin with the following question. 'Who has been significant in my life?' Your response to this would be a list of perhaps ten or twelve names. There is no need to limit it to personal acquaintances and you might want to include authors, TV personalities, politicians, or saints who have influenced you in one way or another. However, if you are new to this technique you may find it easier to limit the list to personal acquaintances.

You might well consider it appropriate to seek God's guidance as to which of these personal relationships you should seek to develop in this way. After considering your list you would choose one who seems particularly significant at this moment. Put his or her name at the top of a fresh sheet and write a few words about your relationship with the chosen person. Now sketch a word portrait of the person (concentrating on their character) and draw up an outline of their life history (using your imagination to fill in any serious gaps). If you like, this can be done as a list of chapter headings for their life history.

Now quieten yourself. Concentrate on the person whose life history you have written, and on your relationship with that person. Build up an inner image of the person you are about to address; see them in your mind's eye; feel their presence. When you feel ready, imagine yourself addressing the person and note down what you say in your journal. In your imagination let them respond to what you have said and record their words in your journal. Let the conversation flow from that initial address and response, keeping a written record of all that goes through your mind in the course of the conversation.

When you have written yourself out, reconsider what you have written. Reflect on it in silence and note down your reactions to it. A key point at which I differ from Progoff is that I would stress the practical implications of the dialogue exercise. If the exercise is to be a fruitful way of developing personal relationships it must have practical consequences, otherwise it may just be a form of escapism. As you reflect you can be asking yourself such questions as, 'What are the practical consequences of this dialogue?' 'Is there something I ought to say or write to this person?' 'Is there something I ought to do?'

Before looking at some of the other possible applications of this technique perhaps I should say a word about a particular form of dialogue with people. It is quite possible that some of the people on your list will be dead or otherwise out of touch with you. In such cases the dialogue technique can still be helpful. For example, it may reveal unfinished business to which you must attend or memories which must be healed. It may itself be part of the healing process.

Dialogues with activities

The same procedure can be applied to almost anything else (the only limit is the capacity of your imagination to personalise the different aspects of your life). One fruitful area of exploration might be to use the technique to look at the way you express yourself through your activities, hobbies, projects, job, habits, things you would like to do, hopes, etc.

The starting point for such an exercise would be the usual one of a list (about ten activities which seem of particular significance to you just now). Armed with this list you would choose the most significant item and write a short description of where you now stand in relation to that activity, what you feel about it, etc. As before this could be followed by a list of chapter headings for the history of its development in your life.

Since you are dealing with an impersonal activity, you may find it more difficult to begin the process of dialogue than before. As a preparation for your imaginary conversation you may find it helpful to turn what you have written over in your mind, relaxing and allowing images to well up into your consciousness. What images does the activity evoke? Those images may be used to help you feel that the activity is present as an identifiable entity.

The actual process of dialogue and subsequent reflection is identical to what I have described before. Again I would underline the importance of being aware of practical implications, asking yourself whether there is any action you wish to take as a result of the exercise. However, I would add a word of caution at this point: beware of drastic life-changing actions suggested by doing one or two of these exercises. Major changes of direction (e.g., deciding to change your job) which are suggested by journal keeping exercises are best discussed with one or more mature Christians who can bring other perspectives to bear upon the matter before you do anything irrevocable.

Dialogues with your body

The same procedure applies in this case with the starting point being a list of memories associated with your awareness of your body and its functions.

Any technique which offers us a way of becoming more aware of our physical bodies must be welcome. For far too long western society has been dominated by a predominantly negative attitude to the body. Influential voices in both Roman Catholicism and Protestantism have encouraged us to spiritualise the Christian faith while the formerly very popular philosophy of dualism encouraged us to see matter and mind (or spirit) as mutually exclusive opposites of which only the latter was our concern.

Dialogues with events

Another application of this technique would be to explore the events, situations and circumstances which have been significant in your life: the things that happen to you rather than the things you do.

Dialogues with society

A final category would be that of the social groups to which you belong. This might include clubs and societies, charities, pressure groups, racial and cultural groups, religious organisations, political organisations. It could also cover less precise ideas such as the labels by which society classifies you (e.g., middle-aged, married, father, unemployed, working class, Asian).

Bringing Jesus into the conversation

Since the dialogue technique described above has evolved in a largely secular environment there is nothing explicitly religious about it. It is a neutral technique which may be used in a wide variety of circumstances.

That being the case, there is no reason why the whole procedure should not be modified to make it explicitly Christian. Indeed, if your main reason for keeping a journal is as a record and guide to your personal spiritual pilgrimage there is every reason for you to make some such modifications.

One way to do this would be to place the whole exercise in a context of prayer, sincerely seeking God's guidance as you attempt to understand the people or events which are the subject of the exercise. A further step might be to extend the conversation to include Jesus. Imagine that he is an onlooker as you begin the conversation. Why not invite him to participate? What might he say in these circumstances? How does his participation affect the conversation? Since this adds an extra dimension of complexity to the dialogue exercise it is probably better to gain some familiarity with it before extending it in this way.

SUPPORT GROUPS

I have already commented that spiritual disciplines are by their very nature not exclusively individualistic. Solo spirituality is about as wise as solo mountaineering!

One way of grounding spiritual journal keeping in the real world would be through a support group. I do not know of any spiritual journal keeping support groups in the UK but perhaps someone who reads this book might be inspired to start one.

The basic requirement would be a small group of people who are committed to using their journals as a spiritual discipline. To keep it intimate enough for serious work it should probably consist of not more than ten people. They would be committed to meeting regularly (perhaps one evening a month).

Such meetings would permit the (voluntary) sharing and discussion of extracts from the members' journals. They would also be opportunities to trade journal keeping tips, pray together, socialise, or work on group exercises (as seemed appropriate). A good place to begin looking for suitable group exercises would be in George Simons' book, *Keeping Your Personal Journal*, which contains a series of exercises with instructions for group use. Other potential resources for such group work may be found in the appendix.

While not strictly connected with ways of making your personal journal more outward-looking, the topic of community and family journals seems to fit more naturally in this chapter than elsewhere.

The family journal

Obviously the main function of such a journal will be different from that of a personal journal. Here we are not interested in charting our own personal and spiritual pilgrimage. It is a public document not a private one: a chronicle of the events which are significant in family life. In fact, many families already keep a rudimentary form of journal in their family photograph albums.

What should it contain? Recalling my advice in chapter 2, I would simply say, 'Whatever you want to put in it'. Photos of important family occasions, certainly; but it may also contain letters, cards, anecdotes, works of art created by the children (or parents), quotable quotes from family members. In fact, it exists as a repository for anything which, in your opinion, reflects, expresses, celebrates, evokes or strengthens the identity of your family.

Instead of daily entries, it might be more appropriate for the entries to be limited to special occasions: birthdays, anniversaries, David's first day at school, Jane's confirmation, Dad's retirement, etc. If you like, you could create a family tradition that the one who is the centre of attention gets to write (or draw)

108

the entry that day. Alternatively you may prefer to have one official chronicler to whom other members of the family could refer any items they wanted to have included in the journal.

Clearly such a journal is a much larger affair than a personal journal. In order to accommodate such things as children's paintings you will need the largest possible loose-leaf binder (A4 or bigger).

The church family journal

There is no reason why a church (or housegroup) should not use a very similar approach to express its identity. In order to keep the journal down to manageable proportions it will probably be necessary to elect a chronicler (or journal editor) to take charge of the journal. They could have the responsibility to beg for suitable materials or, alternatively, edit the masses of unsolicited contributions down.

In these days of high technology it is even possible for a church (or wealthy individuals) to keep a video journal. The parish to which I belong has recently begun to keep a video record of important events within its life (e.g., the church family outing). Again this could be the responsibility of an individual with appropriate gifts or it could be the joint production of several people each adding their own video sequences and commentary.

Exercises

(i) Body maps

As a first step away from self-analysis and introspection, here is a graphical exercise designed to help you get in touch with your bodily experiences.

Begin by relaxing. Gradually allow yourself to become aware of your body.

On a fresh page in your journal, draw a sketch of your body. Record your feelings about being asked to do this. What are your general reactions to the sketch you have produced?

Now mark on your sketch the places where you usually feel energy, excitement, tension, awkwardness, pain, anxiety, or embarrassment. Write about each of these in turn.

Take a few minutes to reflect on what you have written and drawn. Has anything surprised you? Does it have any implications for action you might want to take?

This exercise can be a continuous one. In this case you could carry the sketch as an insert at the current page of your journal, using it to make notes about your bodily experiences over a period of time.

(ii) Celebrate a tree!

This is a simple journal exercise which can also be the basis for worshipping God as creator.

Begin by locating a tree. This may require some effort on the part of city dwellers but most people do, in fact, live within walking distance of a tree.

Make yourself comfortable next to the tree and relax. If you are doing this as part of an act of worship, take time to become aware of God's presence within (and beyond) everything around you.

Turn your attention to the tree. Use your sight to study and enjoy its trunk, its branches, its leaves, its flowers or fruit. Revel in their colours, shapes, textures, and movements.

Listen to the tree. Can you hear the sound of the leaves and branches swaying in the breeze? On a windy day you may be able to hear the creaking of trunk and roots. What about all the animals that make their homes in the tree? Listen for the song of birds and the hum of insects.

Touch the tree. Notice the different sensations of the bark and the leaves against your skin. Is it warm or cool to the touch?

Record your reactions to each of these experiences. If you are doing this as an act of worship, use your reactions and your notes as the basis for an expression of your thanksgiving and praise to God who has given you so much to enjoy.

(iii) Them and us

This simple listing exercise is a way of exposing some of the prejudices and assumptions with which we tend to categorise people.

Relax and spend about ten minutes considering the distinctions (social, religious, racial, etc.) which structure your world. Express them in the form of two lists: those groups of which you are a part (us), and those who are excluded by those groups, the outcasts (them). Continue listing until no more distinctions present themselves to you.

Beginning with the distinction which currently seems most important to you, describe the feelings and events you associate with each distinction.

Take time to reflect on your lists and the associated notes. What does the 'Us' list tell you about yourself? Are you conscious of any prejudices in your attitudes?

(iv) Where am I in relation to the church?

In this exercise, a drawing or diagram is used as the basis for thinking about a particular set of relationships.

As usual begin by relaxing. Ask God to guide your reflections on the church and your place within it.

Spend a few minutes drawing a picture or diagram which describes your local church. Place yourself in the diagram in a position which reflects your place in the life of the church.

Take some time to reflect on what you have drawn, making notes on some of the following questions. What does the picture reveal about the life of the church and your place within it? Who do you relate to within the congregation? What are your feelings about those relationships? Do you feel included or excluded? Where does God figure in the life of the church? Do your relationships within the church help or hinder or seem irrelevant to your relationship with God?

7

Reviewing Your Journal

I hope you will have discovered through doing the exercises in the previous chapters that writing about your personal experiences can be a valuable discipline. In fact, for some journal keepers the initial act of writing out what they think and feel is the most important part of the whole exercise.

However, for most of us the full value of the journal only becomes apparent on rereading. Most journal keepers do, in fact, reread what they have written. They may do so systematically, or they may dip into old volumes more or less at random. They may do so with a specific purpose in mind (why did I make that decision?), or they may do so out of curiosity (what was I doing this time five years ago?).

As the volumes of journals accumulate they form an invaluable archive of your life. As this archive grows, it helps you to gain a sense of the continuity and the patterns of your life: it enables you to perceive the workings of providence. It offers you evidence of personal growth and is thus a source of great encouragement in an age which tends to overlook slow growth in favour of instant results.

When to reread

As with virtually every other aspect of journal keeping there are no rules about when to reread your journal. The best advice is simply to experiment until you find what suits your own personality and way of life.

At one extreme there is the journal keeper who dips into his or her journal irregularly. Perhaps it is a wet Sunday afternoon. What better than to curl up in front of the fire with a good book? Why not the book of your own life?

The other extreme would be the journal keeper who makes a discipline of rereading specific parts of his journal at specific times. Some people like to reread the entries for the preceding day or week before making a new entry in their journal. Others like to know what they were doing on the same day last year. One American advocate of journal keeping as a spiritual discipline sees the regular revision of his journal as an important part of the Christian discipline of self-examination. In addition to a weekly review, he sets time aside for monthly and annual reviews. Anyone who is interested in the possibilities of the journal as a tool for self-examination will probably want to review their entries on a more or less regular basis. For many people the easiest approach to regular revision would probably be to set aside a short period each week to look back over what they have been entering in their journal. Others may prefer to set aside an occasional day or weekend for a more extensive examination of the contents of their journal. Amongst other things, such regular revision of recent journal entries may help you to spot dream patterns, make you more aware of your current concerns and alert you to issues you have been avoiding.

Between these extremes there is an endless variety of possibilities, the common factor being the finding of appropriate times to set your life in a larger context. For some journal keepers the journal itself sets the time. For example, Tristine Rainer likes to review her journal at the end of each volume. Her journal plays such an important role in her life that the start of a new volume takes on a certain mystique. She spends some time reflecting on the way her life has developed during the period defined by the previous volume and considering the developments she would like to see in the next. Those wishes are then summarised in the title she gives to the new volume. Personally, that approach leaves me cold. The idea that the title of your journal might influence your life reminds me of the Victorian repetition of, 'Every day, in every way, I am getting better and better.' Besides, there is no clearly defined end to each volume of my loose-leaf journal. However, setting aside the element of superstition, people who keep a hardback journal may find the end of a volume a convenient time to review what they have been writing.

Another possibility would be to review your journal at the beginning of a new year. This, of course, could simply be identical to Rainer's end of volume approach if you happened to be using a dated journal. Nor is there anything to stop you choosing other dates which seem particularly appropriate or significant to you, e.g., your birthday, wedding anniversary, or a work-related date such as the beginning of the academic year.

My own preferred approach to the rereading of

journals is a variation on that suggested by Ira Progoff. Instead of fixing the rereading by reference to the calendar or other external factors he recommends that you do so at the end of 'subjective life periods'. In other words, it is particularly appropriate to reread your journal at times of rapid change or transition. We have already touched on this in connection with decision making. By putting this time of uncertainty into a larger context, rereading your journal certainly helps in any decisions you have to make. But, at least as important as its pragmatic value is its ability to provide you with a degree of stability at such times. Obvious candidates for such periods of journal revision would include changes of home or job, marriage or other major changes in your personal relationships, illness or bereavement. In fact, any situation or set of circumstances (whether positive or negative) which is causing you stress is a potential indicator that it is time to start rereading the story of your life.

Preparing to reread

Whatever you decide about the time for rereading your journal, it is good to prepare yourself for the task. Such preparation need not be elaborate. The simple act of relaxing before you begin will help you read with full attention and, hence, get more out of your journal. At the very least, making an effort to relax will help you tear your mind away from the immediate pressures of everyday living.

As part of your preparation it may also be helpful to think about your purpose in rereading your journal at this particular time. There are so many possible reasons for rereading that clarifying your current concerns may be helpful in preventing you from getting sidetracked. Generally speaking, reading with a specific purpose or question in mind is a great aid to getting the most out of your journal (or any other written matter). For example, you may decide to review all your records of dreams over a specific period. Or you may reread with a special interest in all references to a particular relationship, or activity, or experience.

It may also be helpful at this stage to set aside a little time to skim through the selected portions of your journal. This initial rapid reading may alert you to striking features which you had not previously noticed. It may help you to spot important issues you had overlooked.

Whatever else you do, make sure you allow yourself sufficient time to read all the relevant material. The sheer size of a journal that has accumulated over several years means that preparation for rereading is essential. How much material do you want to read? Can you do it in one evening or will it be necessary to set aside longer to give yourself the time needed to tackle it without hurrying?

Finally, for anyone using their journal as a spiritual discipline, it is appropriate to set such rereading in a context of prayer. In particular, you may find it helpful to seek God's aid in discerning important issues that are buried in the pages of your journal.

Active rereading

The secret is never to reread your journal passively. It is not a novel in which you can simply let yourself be carried along by the author as he or she unfolds a carefully worked-out story-line. It is more like a collection of scrappy notes, disjointed, contradictory, perhaps even unintelligible. It is raw material from which you may be able to construct something. But the onus is on you to do something as you read. Don't expect your journal to yield treasures without some effort on your part.

What do I mean by active rereading? In an academic context it might be called critical reading. However, to many people that suggests something negative or destructive. Active reading is simply the activity of reading with a purpose (or a set of questions) in mind. It follows naturally from the sort of preparation I described above. It may also involve any of the journal exercises given earlier in the book.

Looking for trends in your journal

The journal is a valuable archive from which to glean information about your behaviour patterns. Things to look out for in this connection would include recurring references to a particular problem. Is it beginning to obsess you? What positive action can you take to deal with it?

Alternatively, you might decide to focus on your references to a particular emotion or feeling. In what circumstances does it appear? If it is negative, can you avoid the situations which seem to give rise to it? If positive, can you do anything to encourage it?

Does your journal contain any negative habits of thought? For example, is guilt or self-blame a regular feature of your entries? If so, an examination of the immediate context of those entries may give you insights into the circumstances which give rise to such thoughts.

On reflection, does the tone of your journal entries seem to be whining at times? Do you seem to complain a lot? Do some entries appear to be emotional over-reactions? Again the journal may give us clues as to what triggers off such responses in us. It may be that some of these entries have tapped hidden depths within your personality. According to Transactional Analysis we all contain an inner child. The influence of this dimension of the personality may be responsible for journal entries whose tone appears to be demanding or excessively emotional.

More generally, it may be worth listening for 'voices' in your journal. Does this entry reflect your conscious self? Or does it express what is expected of you by family, friends, or society at large? Perhaps it is not identifiable as either of these. I have already referred to the inner child. Another possible 'voice' is that of your inner parent: the judgemental dimension of your personality. It may betray itself by the appearance of judgemental expressions, imperatives, words like 'should' and 'ought', and absolutes (e.g., 'always', 'never'). The realm of the unconscious is a rich source for such 'voices' and it may be that you cannot identify it beyond recognising that it does not represent your conscious self. Whatever the source of the 'voice', the dialogue techniques described in earlier chapters may be helpful in getting to know and understand it better.

Another thing to watch for would be records of minor physical ailments (e.g., headaches or upset stomachs). When do they occur? Are there any discernible patterns in their appearance? You may discover a connection between them and a particular relationship or activity. If so, you could use your journal to reflect on why you respond in that way to that situation.

I hope you won't get the impression from what I have just said that such searching for trends is largely negative. On the contrary, it is equally well suited to examining the positive aspects of your life.

For example, you could focus on the pleasurable experiences recorded in your journal. What, in fact, gives you pleasure? To what extent do these differ from the things which society in general and the groups to which you belong say you should find pleasure in? The educationist John Holt refers to a highly educated young man who realised that what really gave him pleasure was carpentry and who had the courage to set up in business as a carpenter against all the expectations society has of someone with multiple university degrees. I don't know if that man kept a journal but his discovery that carpentry was what gave him the greatest pleasure is precisely the sort of thing rereading a journal could reveal.

Again you could ask yourself what personal strengths are revealed by your journal entries. What are the likeable or laudable features of the person revealed by the journal? In what situations and circumstances do these features appear? Is there anything you can do to encourage such situations?

In this way you could run through the entire spectrum of your experiences and relationships looking for patterns and trends in your expression of wholeness, well-being, a sense of achievement or success, happiness, etc.

Another more specialised search for patterns and rhythms in your journal would be to examine the references to dreams. Do you have any recurring dreams? Can you see any correlation between your dreams and your other journal entries? All the material in chapter 4 on working with your dreams could be helpful while you are reviewing your journal.

Finally, on the borderline between the personal

journal and the appointments diary, is there anything which you have conspicuously avoided? Are you procrastinating about something? Reviewing your personal journal may well form the basis for a list of things which need to be attended to.

Examining your writing

Quite apart from the themes which recur in your journal, you may find that your style of writing and even your choice of words has something to say to you.

In attempting to describe variations in human personality, Jung defined four psychological functions: sensing, intuition, thinking and feeling. He believed that while we make use of all four we do so according to a personal hierarchy of preference. It seems likely that the content of our journal will reflect our preference. For example, a tendency to write detailed descriptions may be related to a preference for the sensing function. Similarly, passages of objective rational reflection suggest that the thinking function is in use. By noting the sort of material in our journal we may get a better idea of our own preference amongst the psychological functions. We may find that one or more of the functions is conspicuous by its absence. This might prompt us to ask questions about why we are avoiding that type of writing. For example, why am I reluctant to express my feelings in the journal? Once aware of such preferences we may go on to exercise those neglected functions in our journal keeping.

While on the subject of style, it may be worth considering the vocabulary you use in various circumstances. For example, since we are dealing with personal journals, it would be reasonable to expect the word 'I' to appear fairly frequently. If it does not, it would be worth asking yourself why not? Is it, perhaps, a way of avoiding personal responsibility for what you have written or done? Of course it might be nothing more than a deliberate choice to write in the third person (an approach which used to be quite common).

What about apparent slips of the pen or misspellings? There is such a thing as a Freudian slip. Of course, I am not suggesting that you should check your spelling as if every mistake was of significance. But you may occasionally be struck by the appropriateness of a mistake. For example, I once read an exam script which referred to 'chemystery'! The pupil who made that mistake could not have expressed his feelings for the subject more clearly if he had tried.

Finally even your handwriting may have something to say. There is no need to delve into the esoteric realms of graphology to realise that this is the case. Simply look at the way your handwriting changes in response to different emotional and physical situations. Have sections been written in haste or apparently under pressure? Does your handwriting degenerate to the point of illegibility at times? Or does it sometimes seem cramped? Any features like that may be worth thinking about, particularly if they are associated with particular issues or themes in your journal.

Indexing

It is very helpful to devise some sort of indexing system for use at the initial review stage. At the very least such a system will make subsequent reviews more efficient. A variety of approaches is to be found in the literature on keeping journals.

The most ambitious approach is certainly that of Ira Progoff. In a sense his entire journal keeping system is a way of indexing or classifying journal entries according to a particular theory of mental activity. However, as I commented earlier, what such a classification offers in the way of systematisation is counterbalanced by a severe loss of continuity. It is also worth noting that unless you have a good deal of time to spare for copying out ambiguous material several times to insert into different sections such systematising tends to oversimplify what is actually taking place.

A simpler and more realistic approach is that of George Simons. He recommends a system of marginal letter codes which works equally well with loose-leaf or hardback notebooks. My own version of this approach is as follows:

A: ACTION. This marks any entry which reminds me of things I must do, people I must talk to, etc.

I: IDEA. Entries which offer new perspectives, themes which might be worked out in articles, books, etc.

P: PROBLEM. These are the unresolved problems in my life, issues that I must think about further, and which might be helped by the journal keeping exercises described in the previous chapter.

Pr: PRAYER. This draws attention to entries where I have shifted from my usual descriptive style into some form of address to God.

M: MEDITATIONS. This referred to reflections on biblical and other texts. In fact it no longer appears in my personal journal because, as I mentioned in chapter 2, I happen to find it easier to keep such material separate from my journal.

V: VOICES. These are entries which I regard as unrepresentative of my conscious self. They are the voices of my unconscious.

D: DREAMS. In addition to marking the dream I tend to give it a short descriptive title. Such titles can be listed at the back of your journal to create a dream index.

F: FANTASIES or daydreams. I distinguish these from dreams because they tend to be more deliberate.

R: REVIEW. These entries are ones that I have written as a direct result of reviewing earlier entries.

If such a system seems likely to help you, you could start by modifying the above to suit your own needs. However, I would caution against starting with a complex system. It is far better to begin simply and allow your indexing code to grow with your journal; after all, it is intended to pick out items that are important to you.

Editing and annotating

As I pointed out in chapter 2, the basic rule about editing your journal is, 'Don't!' Reviewing is not the same as revision or editing. You may find yourself two years on, cringeing with embarrassment or self-disgust at past entries. You may find yourself disagreeing strongly with former opinions. The temptation to deny the feelings and opinions of your former self is just as much a temptation to self-delusion as the temptation to write for an audience.

However, it is perfectly valid to make it clear just how you have changed. The most effective way of doing this is by making marginal comments. Thus, it is a good idea always to leave a generous margin (this is less important in a loose-leaf journal as you can always insert an extra sheet for comments). If you simply cannot squeeze your comment into the space available, you can write it in the current section of your journal and make a marginal note referring a reader to that page (or date). You may also find it helpful to write such comments in a distinctive colour.

Rereading as a spiritual discipline

A few extra comments are in order for readers whose main interest is in journal keeping as a spiritual discipline.

Reviewing a spiritual journal is probably most beneficial if you do so in conjunction with a rule of life. Some readers may be put off by the legalistic sound of this term. However, its latin root, *regula*, also suggests the idea of a pattern or model. If you like, it is a set of characteristics which summarise your ideal of the Christian life. It should certainly not be a set of rules the keeping of which enables you to regard yourself as having 'arrived' spiritually.

In fact, most if not all Christians have such a model. For some, that model is Jesus. Others may take a Christian leader of the past or present as their model. Still others look to other members of their congregation. All Christian traditions set up certain standards of behaviour for their adherents. Evangelical churches encourage their members to attend church regularly, engage in daily prayer and Bible reading, join a housegroup, and give a certain amount of their income to support the Church's ministry. A written rule simply spells out certain patterns of behaviour which you seek to emulate.

But what should such a rule look like? In the exercise at the end of this chapter I suggest one possible framework. However, the possibilities are endless. The chapter headings of almost any book on the Christian life could provide you with the framework for a personal rule of life.

A rule of life offers you a ready-made set of questions with which to approach your journal. Are there items in your rule which do not appear in your journal? If so, it would be worth thinking about the reasons for this discrepancy. Why do you not write about them? Are they perhaps less important to you than their appearance in your rule would suggest?

Have you recorded 'violations' of your rule? How do you feel about them? Do you feel guilty? Do you feel a sense of failure? I think it was Martin Thornton who said, 'Rule without fault is of no importance whatsoever.' The purpose of a rule is not success but movement towards an ideal. Since I tend to react in this way, I inserted the following quotation at the very beginning of my rule of life 'The purpose of a rule is to create a profound unity for him who perseveres, who is ready to give up perpetual discussion, and make a fresh beginning again and again' (Roger Schutz).

Conclusion

How should I conclude a revision session? It is only too easy to allow yourself to be carried away by the memories evoked as you reread your journal. Thus it is wise to set a definite time for ending (perhaps setting an alarm clock to remind you).

At the close of the session it is worth taking five

minutes or so to make notes on your reaction to revising the journal. What insights have you gleaned? What emotions has it evoked? What encouragement have you gained from it? This summary could then form the basis for a brief period of prayer (giving thanks for what you have discovered of yourself, asking God's guidance about the action you should take as a result, etc.).

JOURNALLING AND RETREATS

Closely related to the idea of reviewing your journal in order to gain an overview of a period of your life is the traditional Christian notion of a retreat. Some Christians object to the notion because it sounds negative. The word 'retreat' has overtones of escape or withdrawal. There is some truth in that. A retreat *is* an escape, but it is an escape with a purpose.

The reason for withdrawing from the pressures of everyday life for a period of a few days or weeks is simply to give you time to re-collect the scattered fragments of your life. Furthermore, it is an act of re-collection carried out in the presence of God. It is a relatively unstructured period, a space in your life when you can be alone with God. As such it may actually be a very disturbing time: a time when all the little comforts and securities of everyday life are stripped away.

Your journal is a valuable companion at such times. For some people (myself included) it is a very helpful aid to concentration. Without it I would find that my mind rapidly begins to wander over all sorts of irrelevancies. It also offers a way of recording any insights or spiritual experiences which might occur during the retreat. In fact, some Christians find that they do most of their journal keeping while they are on retreat. A good example of a modern retreat journal would be Henri Nouwen's *Genesee Diary*.

In theory, it would be possible to base an entire retreat on the practice of journal keeping, using journal keeping exercises in place of more traditional forms of spiritual exercise. Such retreats can be found in the United States but, to the best of my knowledge, they have not yet crossed to this side of the Atlantic (do not confuse them with journal keeping workshops, which are to be found in the UK but which are much more intense than any retreat).

Exercise

Creating a rule of life

I spoke above of using a rule of life to guide your rereading of your journal. It is equally possible to use a revision session to guide your creation of a rule of life.

A simple rule of life might include paragraphs about each of the following: public worship, self-examination, personal prayer (perhaps, including an annual retreat), study, life-style, and work. After a suitable period of preparation, read through the chosen period in your journal with each of these headings in mind. Use the memories evoked by your journal and any other insights that come to you as you read as the basis for a short statement summarising what you would regard as a realistic pattern of Christian living for you to follow.

However, before attempting to put any such rule into practice, it would certainly be worthwhile to discuss it with a mature Christian. In this way you lessen the risk of setting yourself unrealistic targets.

Or, you may find that talking it through with someone else brings to your attention aspects of Christian spirituality and living which you had overlooked.

Appendix: Further Resources

BOOKS ABOUT JOURNALS AND JOURNAL KEEPING

England, Edward (ed.), *Keeping a Spiritual Journal*. Crowborough, Highland Books, 1988.

Kelsey, Morton, *Adventure Inwards: Christian Growth Through Personal Journal Writing*. Minneapolis, Augsburg Publishing House, 1980.

Mallon, Thomas, *A Book of One's Own: People and Their Diaries*. London, Pan, 1985.

Milner, Marion, *An Experiment in Leisure*. London, Virago Press, 1986.

A Life of One's Own. London, Virago Press, 1986.

Eternity's Sunrise: A Way of Keeping a Diary. London, Virago Press, 1987.

Progoff, Ira, *At a Journal Workshop*. New York, Dialogue House, 1977.

The Practice of Process Meditation. New York, Dialogue House, 1980.

Rainer, Tristine, *The New Diary*. London, Angus & Robertson, 1980.

Simons, George F., *Keeping Your Personal Journal*. New York, Paulist Press, 1978.

SOME PUBLISHED JOURNALS (FACT AND FICTION)

Brainerd, David, *The Life and Diary*. Chicago, Moody Press, 1980.

Darwin, Charles, *The Voyage of the 'Beagle'*. London, Dent, 1972.

Elliott, Elisabeth (ed.), *The Journals of Jim Elliott*. London, Pickering & Inglis, 1979.

Fox, George, *Journal*, 2 vols. New York, Octagon Books, 1973.

Frank, Anne, *The Diary*. London, Pan, 1968.

Gide, André, *Journals 1889–1949*. Harmondsworth, Penguin, 1967.

Hammarskjöld, Dag, *Markings*. London, Faber, 1964.

Hillesum, Etty, *Etty: A Diary 1941–43*. London, Granada.

Kierkegaard, Søren, *The Journals 1834–1854*. London, Fontana, 1958.

The Last Years: Journals 1853–55. London, Fontana, 1968.

Kilvert, Francis, *Kilvert's Diary: A Selection*. Harmondsworth, Penguin, 1977.

Lewis, C. S., *A Grief Observed*. London, Faber, 1966.

Mansfield, Katherine, *Letters and Journal*. Harmondsworth, Penguin, 1977.

Merton, Thomas, *The Asian Journal*. London, Sheldon Press, 1975.

The Secular Journal. London, Sheldon Press, 1977.

Nin, Anaïs, *The Diary*, 7 vols. New York, Harcourt, Brace & Jovanovich, 1978.

Nouwen, Henri, *The Genesee Diary*. New York, Doubleday, 1981.

The Road to Daybreak: A Spiritual Journey. London, Darton, Longman & Todd, 1989.

Plass, Adrian, *The Sacred Diary of Adrian Plass, Aged 37¾*. London, Marshall-Pickering, 1987.

Potter, Beatrix, *Journal, 1881–1893* (abridged). London, Frederick Warne, 1966.

Roncalli, Angelo [Pope John XXIII], *Journal of a Soul*. London, New English Library, 1966.

Talbot, John Michael, *Changes*. New York, Crossroad, 1987.

Thoreau, Henry, *Selected Journals*. New York, New American Library, 1982.

Townsend, Sue, *The Secret Diary of Adrian Mole, Aged 13¾*. London, Methuen, 1982.

Wesley, John, *The Journal* (abridged). Chicago, Moody Press, 1974.

Whitefield, George, *Journals*. Edinburgh, Banner of Truth, 1978.

Woodforde, James, *The Diary of a Country Parson* (abridged). Oxford, OUP, 1949.

Woolman, John, *The Journal*. Secaucus, NJ, Citadel Press, 1972.

OTHER BOOKS

The following books about Christian spirituality contain material relevant to the suggestions I have made and/or exercises which may be adapted for use in a journal.

Dewar, Francis, *Live for a Change*. London, Darton, Longman & Todd, 1988.

Hughes, Gerard, W., *God of Surprises*. London, Darton, Longman & Todd, 1985.

Link, Mark, *You: Prayer For Beginners and Those Who Have Forgotten How*. Niles, Ill., Argus, 1976.

McAlpine, Campbell, *The Practice of Biblical Meditation*. London, Marshall, Morgan & Scott, 1981.
de Mello, Anthony, *Sadhana: A Way to God*. New York, Doubleday, 1978.
  Wellsprings: A Book of Spiritual Exercises. Anand, India, Gujarat Sahitya Prakash, 1984.
Parker, Russ, *Dreams and Spirituality*. Bramcote, Grove Books, 1985.
Pooley, Roger, *Spiritual Autobiography: A DIY Guide*. Bramcote, Grove Books, 1983.
Puhl, Louis (tr.), *The Spiritual Exercises of St Ignatius*. Chicago, Loyola University Press, 1951.

JOURNAL KEEPING WORKSHOPS

Information is obtainable from:
Emmaus House, Clifton Hill, Clifton, Bristol BS8 4PD.
Inigo Centre, Southwell House, 39 Fitzjohns Avenue, London, NW3 5JT.
National Retreat Centre, Liddon House, 24 South Audley Street, London, W1Y 5DL.
Post Green Community, 56 Dorchester Rd., Lytchett Minster, Poole, Dorset, BH16 6JE.